MIND
CANDY
MINUTE

JOURNAL

If found, please contact:
_____
_____
_____

Created by
Felicia Pizzonia

Copyright © 2018 by Ultimate Publishing House.

All rights reserved as this book may not be reproduced in whole or in part, by any means, without written consent of the publisher. For permission requests, write to the publisher, addressed "Attention: Permissions Coordinator" at the address below.

THE ULTIMATE PUBLISHING HOUSE (UPH) US HEADQUARTERS
P.O. Box 1204, Cypress, Texas, U.S.A. 77410

Canadian Office: 205 Glen Shields Avenue, Toronto, Ontario, Canada L4K 2B0
Telephone: 647-883-1758

MIND CANDY MINUTE JOURNAL
www.ultimatepublishinghouse.com
www.MindCandyBook.com
www.FeliciaPizzonia.com
E-mail: info@ultimatepublishinghouse.com

US OFFICE: Ordering Information

Quantity Sales: COMPANIES, ORGANIZATIONS, INSTITUTIONS, AND INDUSTRY PUBLICATIONS.

Quantity discounts are available on bulk purchases of this book for reselling, educational purposes, subscription incentives, gifts, sponsorship, or fundraising. Unique books or book excerpts can also be fashioned to suit special needs such as private labeling with your logo on the cover and a message from or a message printed on the second page of the book. For more information, please contact our Special Sales Department at Ultimate Publishing House. Orders for college textbook or course adoption use.

Please contact Ultimate Publishing House Tel: 647-883-1758

Ultimate Publishing House - Printed in the United States

Mind Candy Journal, by Felicia Pizzonia

ISBN-978-1-7325389-8-6

To all the incredible humans in this world whom have dedicated their lives to learning and contributing. You change the world one day at a time!

The importance of repetition until automaticity cannot be overstated. Repetition is the key to learning.

—JOHN WOODEN

The Mind Candy Minute Journal is the ultimate way to train your mind by writing / penning your goals, dreams and aspirations & fuelling them with a flow of gratitude. Take massive action, create the magic and watch miracles unfold. The journal will guide you.

My Mind Candy Minute Journal

Date ____/____/_____

"Anything in life worth having is worth working for." - Andrew Carnegie

I am grateful for...

1. _____
2. _____
3. _____

Daily affirmations. Mind Candy Voice Note *(Record your affirmations on your smart phone and listen to them several times throughout your day)*

I am... _____

_____

_____

_____

_____

_____

_____

My two massive goals to focus on today:

1. _____
2. _____

Take three deep "oxytocin breaths" by placing your hand on your heart and exhaling the sound "haaaaa".

My Mind Candy Minute Journal

Date ____/____/_____

"Success often comes to those who dare to act. It seldom goes to the timid who are ever afraid of the consequences." - Jawaharlal Nehru

I am grateful for...

1. _____
2. _____
3. _____

Daily affirmations. Mind Candy Voice Note *(Record your affirmations on your smart phone and listen to them several times throughout your day)*

I am... _____
_____
_____
_____
_____
_____
_____

My two massive goals to focus on today:

1. _____
2. _____

Take three deep "oxytocin breaths" by placing your hand on your heart and exhaling the sound "haaaaa".

My Mind Candy Minute Journal

Date ____/____/_____

"Success is never ending, failure is never final." - Dr. Robert Schuller

I am grateful for...

1. _____
2. _____
3. _____

Daily affirmations. Mind Candy Voice Note *(Record your affirmations on your smart phone and listen to them several times throughout your day)*

I am... _____

_____
_____
_____
_____
_____
_____

My two massive goals to focus on today:

1. _____
2. _____

Take three deep "oxytocin breaths" by placing your hand on your heart and exhaling the sound "haaaaa".

My Mind Candy Minute Journal

Date ____/____/_____

"I just love when people say I can't do something because all my life people said I wasn't going to make it." - Ted Turner

I am grateful for...

1. _____
2. _____
3. _____

Daily affirmations. Mind Candy Voice Note *(Record your affirmations on your smart phone and listen to them several times throughout your day)*

I am... _____

_____

_____

_____

_____

_____

_____

My two massive goals to focus on today:

1. _____
2. _____

Take three deep "oxytocin breaths" by placing your hand on your heart and exhaling the sound "haaaaa".

My Mind Candy Minute Journal

Date ____/____/_____

"Great thoughts speak only to the thoughtful mind, but great actions speak to all mankind." - Emily P. Bissell

I am grateful for...

1. _____
2. _____
3. _____

Daily affirmations. Mind Candy Voice Note *(Record your affirmations on your smart phone and listen to them several times throughout your day)*

I am... _____

_____
_____
_____
_____
_____
_____

My two massive goals to focus on today:

1. _____
2. _____

Take three deep "oxytocin breaths" by placing your hand on your heart and exhaling the sound "haaaaa".

My Mind Candy Minute Journal

Date ____/____/_____

"Obstacles are those frightful things you can see when you take your eyes off your goal." - Henry Ford

I am grateful for...

1. _____
2. _____
3. _____

Daily affirmations. Mind Candy Voice Note *(Record your affirmations on your smart phone and listen to them several times throughout your day)*

I am... _____

_____
_____
_____
_____
_____
_____

My two massive goals to focus on today:

1. _____
2. _____

Take three deep "oxytocin breaths" by placing your hand on your heart and exhaling the sound "haaaaa".

My Mind Candy Minute Journal

Date ____/____/_____

"It takes a strong fish to swim against the current. Even a dead one can float with it." - John Crowe

I am grateful for...

1. _____
2. _____
3. _____

Daily affirmations. Mind Candy Voice Note *(Record your affirmations on your smart phone and listen to them several times throughout your day)*

I am... _____
_____
_____
_____
_____
_____

My two massive goals to focus on today:

1. _____
2. _____

Take three deep "oxytocin breaths" by placing your hand on your heart and exhaling the sound "haaaaa".

My Mind Candy Minute Journal

Date ____/____/_____

"You will never find time for anything. You must make it." - Charles Buxton

I am grateful for...

1. _____
2. _____
3. _____

Daily affirmations. Mind Candy Voice Note *(Record your affirmations on your smart phone and listen to them several times throughout your day)*

I am... _____
_____
_____
_____
_____
_____
_____
_____

My two massive goals to focus on today:

1. _____
2. _____

Take three deep "oxytocin breaths" by placing your hand on your heart and exhaling the sound "haaaaa".

My Mind Candy Minute Journal

Date _____/_____/_____

"Remove failure as an option." - Joan Lunden

I am grateful for...

1. _____
2. _____
3. _____

Daily affirmations. Mind Candy Voice Note *(Record your affirmations on your smart phone and listen to them several times throughout your day)*

I am... _____

_____

_____

_____

_____

_____

_____

My two massive goals to focus on today:

1. _____
2. _____

Take three deep "oxytocin breaths" by placing your hand
on your heart and exhaling the sound "haaaaa".

My Mind Candy Minute Journal

Date ____/____/_____

*"There is no one giant step that does it. It's a
lot of little steps." - Peter A. Cohen*

I am grateful for...

1. _____
2. _____
3. _____

Daily affirmations. Mind Candy Voice Note *(Record your affirmations on your smart phone and listen to them several times throughout your day)*

I am... _____
_____
_____
_____
_____
_____
_____

My two massive goals to focus on today:

1. _____
2. _____

Take three deep "oxytocin breaths" by placing your hand
on your heart and exhaling the sound "haaaaa".

My Mind Candy Minute Journal

Date ____/____/_____

"Shoot for the moon. Even if you miss, you will land among the stars." - Les Brown

I am grateful for...

1. _____
2. _____
3. _____

Daily affirmations. Mind Candy Voice Note *(Record your affirmations on your smart phone and listen to them several times throughout your day)*

I am... _____

_____
_____
_____
_____
_____
_____

My two massive goals to focus on today:

1. _____
2. _____

Take three deep "oxytocin breaths" by placing your hand on your heart and exhaling the sound "haaaaa".

My Mind Candy Minute Journal

Date ____/____/_____

"Some of us have great runways already built for us. If you have one, take off. But if you don't have one, realize it is your responsibility to grab a shovel and build one for yourself and for those who will follow after you." - Amelia Earhart

I am grateful for...

1. _____
2. _____
3. _____

Daily affirmations. Mind Candy Voice Note *(Record your affirmations on your smart phone and listen to them several times throughout your day)*

I am... _____

_____
_____
_____
_____
_____
_____

My two massive goals to focus on today:

1. _____
2. _____

Take three deep "oxytocin breaths" by placing your hand on your heart and exhaling the sound "haaaaa".

My Mind Candy Minute Journal

Date ____/____/_____

"Work like you don't need the money. Love like you've never been hurt. Dance like nobody is watching." - Mark Twain

I am grateful for...

1. _____
2. _____
3. _____

Daily affirmations. Mind Candy Voice Note *(Record your affirmations on your smart phone and listen to them several times throughout your day)*

I am... _____

_____

_____

_____

_____

_____

_____

My two massive goals to focus on today:

1. _____
2. _____

Take three deep "oxytocin breaths" by placing your hand on your heart and exhaling the sound "haaaaa".

My Mind Candy Minute Journal

Date ____/____/_____

"What the mind of man can conceive and believe, it can achieve." - Napoleon Hill

I am grateful for...

1. _____
2. _____
3. _____

Daily affirmations. Mind Candy Voice Note *(Record your affirmations on your smart phone and listen to them several times throughout your day)*

I am... _____

_____
_____
_____
_____
_____
_____

My two massive goals to focus on today:

1. _____
2. _____

Take three deep "oxytocin breaths" by placing your hand on your heart and exhaling the sound "haaaaa".

My Mind Candy Minute Journal

Date ____/____/_____

"There are no secrets to success. It is the result of preparation, hard work, and learning from failure." - Colin Powell

I am grateful for...

1. _____
2. _____
3. _____

Daily affirmations. Mind Candy Voice Note *(Record your affirmations on your smart phone and listen to them several times throughout your day)*

I am... _____

_____
_____
_____
_____
_____
_____

My two massive goals to focus on today:

1. _____
2. _____

Take three deep "oxytocin breaths" by placing your hand on your heart and exhaling the sound "haaaaa".

My Mind Candy Minute Journal

Date ____/____/_____

"What lies behind us and what lies before us are tiny matters compared to what lies within us." - Ralph Waldo Emerson

I am grateful for...

1. _____
2. _____
3. _____

Daily affirmations. Mind Candy Voice Note *(Record your affirmations on your smart phone and listen to them several times throughout your day)*

I am... _____

_____
_____
_____
_____
_____
_____

My two massive goals to focus on today:

1. _____
2. _____

Take three deep "oxytocin breaths" by placing your hand on your heart and exhaling the sound "haaaaa".

My Mind Candy Minute Journal

Date ____/____/_____

"Great works are performed not by strength but by perseverance." - Samuel Johnson

I am grateful for...

1. _____
2. _____
3. _____

Daily affirmations. Mind Candy Voice Note *(Record your affirmations on your smart phone and listen to them several times throughout your day)*

I am... _____

_____

_____

_____

_____

_____

My two massive goals to focus on today:

1. _____
2. _____

Take three deep "oxytocin breaths" by placing your hand on your heart and exhaling the sound "haaaaa".

My Mind Candy Minute Journal

Date _____/_____/_____

"The difference between a successful person and others is not a lack of strength, not a lack of knowledge, but rather a lack of will." - Vince Lombardi

I am grateful for...

1. _____
2. _____
3. _____

Daily affirmations. Mind Candy Voice Note *(Record your affirmations on your smart phone and listen to them several times throughout your day)*

I am... _____
_____
_____
_____
_____
_____
_____

My two massive goals to focus on today:

1. _____
2. _____

Take three deep "oxytocin breaths" by placing your hand on your heart and exhaling the sound "haaaaa".

My Mind Candy Minute Journal

Date ____/____/_____

"The man who follows the crowd will usually get no further than the crowd. The man who walks alone is likely to find himself in places no one has ever been." - Alan Ashley-Pitt

I am grateful for...

1. _____
2. _____
3. _____

Daily affirmations. Mind Candy Voice Note *(Record your affirmations on your smart phone and listen to them several times throughout your day)*

I am... _____

_____

_____

_____

_____

_____

_____

My two massive goals to focus on today:

1. _____
2. _____

Take three deep "oxytocin breaths" by placing your hand on your heart and exhaling the sound "haaaaa".

My Mind Candy Minute Journal

Date ____/____/_____

"It takes 20 years to build a reputation and five minutes to ruin it. If you think about that, you'll do things differently." - Warren Buffett

I am grateful for...

1. _____
2. _____
3. _____

Daily affirmations. Mind Candy Voice Note *(Record your affirmations on your smart phone and listen to them several times throughout your day)*

I am... _____

_____
_____
_____
_____
_____
_____
_____

My two massive goals to focus on today:

1. _____
2. _____

Take three deep "oxytocin breaths" by placing your hand on your heart and exhaling the sound "haaaaa".

My Mind Candy Minute Journal

Date ____/____/_____

"Champions aren't made in the gyms. Champions are made from something they have deep inside them - a desire, a dream, a vision." - Muhammad Ali

I am grateful for...

1. _____
2. _____
3. _____

Daily affirmations. Mind Candy Voice Note *(Record your affirmations on your smart phone and listen to them several times throughout your day)*

I am... _____

_____
_____
_____
_____
_____
_____

My two massive goals to focus on today:

1. _____
2. _____

Take three deep "oxytocin breaths" by placing your hand on your heart and exhaling the sound "haaaaa".

My Mind Candy Minute Journal

Date ____/____/_____

"Dwell not on the past. Use it to illustrate a point, then leave it behind. Nothing really matters except what you do now in this instant of time. From this moment onwards you can be an entirely different person, filled with love and understanding, ready with an outstretched hand, uplifted and positive in every thought and deed." - Eileen Caddy

I am grateful for...

1. _____
2. _____
3. _____

Daily affirmations. Mind Candy Voice Note *(Record your affirmations on your smart phone and listen to them several times throughout your day)*

I am... _____

_____
_____
_____
_____
_____
_____

My two massive goals to focus on today:

1. _____
2. _____

Take three deep "oxytocin breaths" by placing your hand on your heart and exhaling the sound "haaaaa".

My Mind Candy Minute Journal

Date ____/____/_____

"The critical ingredient is getting off your butt and doing something. It's as simple as that. A lot of people have ideas, but there are few who decide to do something about them now. Not tomorrow. Not next week. But today. The true entrepreneur is a doer." - Nolan Bushnell

I am grateful for...

1. _____
2. _____
3. _____

Daily affirmations. Mind Candy Voice Note *(Record your affirmations on your smart phone and listen to them several times throughout your day)*

I am... _____

_____
_____
_____
_____
_____
_____

My two massive goals to focus on today:

1. _____
2. _____

Take three deep "oxytocin breaths" by placing your hand on your heart and exhaling the sound "haaaaa".

My Mind Candy Minute Journal

Date ____/____/_____

"Whatever you vividly imagine, ardently desire, sincerely believe, and enthusiastically act upon must inevitably come to pass!" - Paul J. Meyer

I am grateful for...

1. _____
2. _____
3. _____

Daily affirmations. Mind Candy Voice Note *(Record your affirmations on your smart phone and listen to them several times throughout your day)*

I am... _____

_____
_____
_____
_____
_____
_____
_____

My two massive goals to focus on today:

1. _____
2. _____

Take three deep "oxytocin breaths" by placing your hand on your heart and exhaling the sound "haaaaa".

My Mind Candy Minute Journal

Date ____/____/_____

"Keep away from small people who try to belittle your ambitions. Small people always do that, but the really great make you feel that you too can become great." - Mark Twain

I am grateful for...

1. _____
2. _____
3. _____

Daily affirmations. Mind Candy Voice Note *(Record your affirmations on your smart phone and listen to them several times throughout your day)*

I am... _____

_____
_____
_____
_____
_____
_____

My two massive goals to focus on today:

1. _____
2. _____

Take three deep "oxytocin breaths" by placing your hand on your heart and exhaling the sound "haaaaa".

My Mind Candy Minute Journal

Date ____/____/_____

"For anything worth having one must pay the price; and the price is always work, patience, love, self-sacrifice. No paper currency, no promises to pay, but the gold of real service." - John Burroughs

I am grateful for...

1. _____
2. _____
3. _____

Daily affirmations. Mind Candy Voice Note *(Record your affirmations on your smart phone and listen to them several times throughout your day)*

I am... _____

_____
_____
_____
_____
_____
_____

My two massive goals to focus on today:

1. _____
2. _____

Take three deep "oxytocin breaths" by placing your hand on your heart and exhaling the sound "haaaaa".

My Mind Candy Minute Journal

Date ____/____/_____

"To be successful, you must decide exactly what you want to accomplish, then resolve to pay the price to get it." - Bunker Hunt

I am grateful for...

1. _____
2. _____
3. _____

Daily affirmations. Mind Candy Voice Note *(Record your affirmations on your smart phone and listen to them several times throughout your day)*

I am... _____

_____
_____
_____
_____
_____
_____

My two massive goals to focus on today:

1. _____
2. _____

Take three deep "oxytocin breaths" by placing your hand on your heart and exhaling the sound "haaaaa".

My Mind Candy Minute Journal

Date ____/____/_____

"You just can't beat the person who never gives up." - Babe Ruth

I am grateful for...

1. _____
2. _____
3. _____

Daily affirmations. Mind Candy Voice Note *(Record your affirmations on your smart phone and listen to them several times throughout your day)*

I am... _____

_____

_____

_____

_____

_____

_____

My two massive goals to focus on today:

1. _____
2. _____

Take three deep "oxytocin breaths" by placing your hand on your heart and exhaling the sound "haaaaa".

My Mind Candy Minute Journal

Date ____/____/_____

"When you get right down to the root of the meaning of the word 'succeed', you find it simply means to follow through." - F.W. Nichol

I am grateful for...

1. _____
2. _____
3. _____

Daily affirmations. Mind Candy Voice Note *(Record your affirmations on your smart phone and listen to them several times throughout your day)*

I am... _____

_____
_____
_____
_____
_____
_____

My two massive goals to focus on today:

1. _____
2. _____

Take three deep "oxytocin breaths" by placing your hand on your heart and exhaling the sound "haaaaa".

My Mind Candy Minute Journal

Date ____/____/_____

"Successful people are always looking for opportunities to help others. Unsuccessful people are always asking, 'What's in it for me?'" - Brian Tracy

I am grateful for...

1. _____
2. _____
3. _____

Daily affirmations. Mind Candy Voice Note *(Record your affirmations on your smart phone and listen to them several times throughout your day)*

I am... _____
_____
_____
_____
_____
_____
_____

My two massive goals to focus on today:

1. _____
2. _____

Take three deep "oxytocin breaths" by placing your hand on your heart and exhaling the sound "haaaaa".

My Mind Candy Minute Journal

Date ____/____/_____

"If you don't set goals, you can't regret not reaching them." - Yogi Berra

I am grateful for...

1. _____
2. _____
3. _____

Daily affirmations. Mind Candy Voice Note *(Record your affirmations on your smart phone and listen to them several times throughout your day)*

I am... _____

_____
_____
_____
_____
_____
_____

My two massive goals to focus on today:

1. _____
2. _____

Take three deep "oxytocin breaths" by placing your hand on your heart and exhaling the sound "haaaaa".

My Mind Candy Minute Journal

Date ____/____/_____

"Success is achieved by those who try and keep trying with a positive mental attitude." - W. Clement Stone

I am grateful for...

1. _____
2. _____
3. _____

Daily affirmations. Mind Candy Voice Note *(Record your affirmations on your smart phone and listen to them several times throughout your day)*

I am... _____

_____
_____
_____
_____
_____
_____

My two massive goals to focus on today:

1. _____
2. _____

Take three deep "oxytocin breaths" by placing your hand on your heart and exhaling the sound "haaaaa".

My Mind Candy Minute Journal

Date ____/____/_____

"I couldn't wait for success, so I went ahead without it." - Jonathan Winters

I am grateful for...

1. _____
2. _____
3. _____

Daily affirmations. Mind Candy Voice Note *(Record your affirmations on your smart phone and listen to them several times throughout your day)*

I am... _____

_____
_____
_____
_____
_____
_____

My two massive goals to focus on today:

1. _____
2. _____

Take three deep "oxytocin breaths" by placing your hand on your heart and exhaling the sound "haaaaa".

My Mind Candy Minute Journal

Date ____/____/_____

"What we hope to do with ease, we must learn first to do with diligence." - Samuel Johnson

I am grateful for...

1. _____
2. _____
3. _____

Daily affirmations. Mind Candy Voice Note *(Record your affirmations on your smart phone and listen to them several times throughout your day)*

I am... _____

_____
_____
_____
_____
_____
_____

My two massive goals to focus on today:

1. _____
2. _____

Take three deep "oxytocin breaths" by placing your hand on your heart and exhaling the sound "haaaaa".

My Mind Candy Minute Journal

Date ____/____/_____

"We do our best that we know how at the moment, and if it doesn't turn out, we modify it." - Franklin Delano Roosevelt

I am grateful for...

1. _____
2. _____
3. _____

Daily affirmations. Mind Candy Voice Note *(Record your affirmations on your smart phone and listen to them several times throughout your day)*

I am... _____

_____
_____
_____
_____
_____
_____

My two massive goals to focus on today:

1. _____
2. _____

Take three deep "oxytocin breaths" by placing your hand on your heart and exhaling the sound "haaaaa".

My Mind Candy Minute Journal

Date ____/____/_____

"A Native American grandfather was talking to his grandson about how he felt. He said, 'I feel as if I have two wolves fighting in my heart. One wolf is the vengeful, violent one, the other wolf is the loving compassionate one.' The grandson asked him, 'Which wolf will win the fight in your heart?' The grandfather answered, 'The one I feed.'" - Blackhawk

I am grateful for...

1. _____
2. _____
3. _____

Daily affirmations. Mind Candy Voice Note *(Record your affirmations on your smart phone and listen to them several times throughout your day)*

I am... _____
_____
_____
_____
_____
_____
_____

My two massive goals to focus on today:

1. _____
2. _____

Take three deep "oxytocin breaths" by placing your hand on your heart and exhaling the sound "haaaaa".

My Mind Candy Minute Journal

Date ____/____/_____

"Enthusiasm is the steam that drives the engine." - Napoleon Hill

I am grateful for...

1. _____
2. _____
3. _____

Daily affirmations. Mind Candy Voice Note *(Record your affirmations on your smart phone and listen to them several times throughout your day)*

I am... _____

_____
_____
_____
_____
_____
_____

My two massive goals to focus on today:

1. _____
2. _____

Take three deep "oxytocin breaths" by placing your hand
on your heart and exhaling the sound "haaaaa".

My Mind Candy Minute Journal

Date ____/____/_____

"The winners in life think constantly in terms of I can, I will, and I am. Losers, on the other hand, concentrate their waking thoughts on what they should have or would have done, or what they can't do." - Dennis Waitley

I am grateful for...

1. _____
2. _____
3. _____

Daily affirmations. Mind Candy Voice Note *(Record your affirmations on your smart phone and listen to them several times throughout your day)*

I am... _____

_____
_____
_____
_____
_____
_____

My two massive goals to focus on today:

1. _____
2. _____

Take three deep "oxytocin breaths" by placing your hand on your heart and exhaling the sound "haaaaa".

My Mind Candy Minute Journal

Date ____/____/_____

"Success in life has nothing to do with what you gain in life or accomplish for yourself. It's what you do for others." - Danny Thomas

I am grateful for...

1. _____
2. _____
3. _____

Daily affirmations. Mind Candy Voice Note *(Record your affirmations on your smart phone and listen to them several times throughout your day)*

I am... _____

_____
_____
_____
_____
_____
_____
_____

My two massive goals to focus on today:

1. _____
2. _____

Take three deep "oxytocin breaths" by placing your hand on your heart and exhaling the sound "haaaaa".

My Mind Candy Minute Journal

Date ____/____/_____

"Empty pockets never held anyone back. Only empty heads and empty hearts can do that." - Norman Vincent Peale

I am grateful for...

1. _____
2. _____
3. _____

Daily affirmations. Mind Candy Voice Note *(Record your affirmations on your smart phone and listen to them several times throughout your day)*

I am... _____

_____
_____
_____
_____
_____
_____

My two massive goals to focus on today:

1. _____
2. _____

Take three deep "oxytocin breaths" by placing your hand on your heart and exhaling the sound "haaaaa".

My Mind Candy Minute Journal

Date ____/____/_____

"One man with courage is a majority." - Andrew Jackson

I am grateful for...

1. _____
2. _____
3. _____

Daily affirmations. Mind Candy Voice Note *(Record your affirmations on your smart phone and listen to them several times throughout your day)*

I am... _____

_____

_____

_____

_____

_____

My two massive goals to focus on today:

1. _____
2. _____

Take three deep "oxytocin breaths" by placing your hand on your heart and exhaling the sound "haaaaa".

My Mind Candy Minute Journal

Date ____/____/_____

"Not many people are willing to give failure a second opportunity. They fail once and it is all over. The bitter pill of failure is often more than most people can handle. If you are willing to accept failure and learn from it, if you are willing to consider failure as a blessing in disguise and bounce back, you have got the essential of harnessing one of the most powerful success forces." - Joseph Sugarman

I am grateful for...

1. _____
2. _____
3. _____

Daily affirmations. Mind Candy Voice Note *(Record your affirmations on your smart phone and listen to them several times throughout your day)*

I am... _____
_____
_____
_____
_____
_____
_____

My two massive goals to focus on today:

1. _____
2. _____

Take three deep "oxytocin breaths" by placing your hand on your heart and exhaling the sound "haaaaa".

My Mind Candy Minute Journal

Date ____/____/_____

"Every achiever I have ever met says, 'My life turned around when I began to believe in me.'" - Robert Schuller

I am grateful for...

1. _____
2. _____
3. _____

Daily affirmations. Mind Candy Voice Note *(Record your affirmations on your smart phone and listen to them several times throughout your day)*

I am... _____

_____
_____
_____
_____
_____
_____

My two massive goals to focus on today:

1. _____
2. _____

Take three deep "oxytocin breaths" by placing your hand on your heart and exhaling the sound "haaaaa".

My Mind Candy Minute Journal

Date ____/____/_____

"I don't measure a man's success by how high he climbs but how high he bounces when he hits bottom." - George Patton

I am grateful for...

1. _____
2. _____
3. _____

Daily affirmations. Mind Candy Voice Note *(Record your affirmations on your smart phone and listen to them several times throughout your day)*

I am... _____

_____
_____
_____
_____
_____
_____

My two massive goals to focus on today:

1. _____
2. _____

Take three deep "oxytocin breaths" by placing your hand on your heart and exhaling the sound "haaaaa".

My Mind Candy Minute Journal

Date ____/____/_____

"One step - choosing a goal and sticking to it - changes everything." - Scott Reed

I am grateful for...

1. _____
2. _____
3. _____

Daily affirmations. Mind Candy Voice Note *(Record your affirmations on your smart phone and listen to them several times throughout your day)*

I am... _____

_____
_____
_____
_____
_____
_____

My two massive goals to focus on today:

1. _____
2. _____

Take three deep "oxytocin breaths" by placing your hand on your heart and exhaling the sound "haaaaa".

My Mind Candy Minute Journal

Date _____/_____/_____

"Dependent people need others to get what they want. Independent people can get what they want through their own efforts. Interdependent people combine their own efforts with the efforts of others to achieve their greatest success." - Stephen Covey

I am grateful for...

1. _____
2. _____
3. _____

Daily affirmations. Mind Candy Voice Note *(Record your affirmations on your smart phone and listen to them several times throughout your day)*

I am... _____

_____
_____
_____
_____
_____
_____

My two massive goals to focus on today:

1. _____
2. _____

Take three deep "oxytocin breaths" by placing your hand on your heart and exhaling the sound "haaaaa".

My Mind Candy Minute Journal

Date ____/____/_____

"I don't know what your destiny will be, but one thing I do know: The only ones among you who will be really happy are those who have sought and found how to serve." - Albert Schweitzer

I am grateful for...

1. _____
2. _____
3. _____

Daily affirmations. Mind Candy Voice Note *(Record your affirmations on your smart phone and listen to them several times throughout your day)*

I am... _____
_____
_____
_____
_____
_____
_____

My two massive goals to focus on today:

1. _____
2. _____

Take three deep "oxytocin breaths" by placing your hand on your heart and exhaling the sound "haaaaa".

My Mind Candy Minute Journal

Date ____/____/_____

"Success is the child of audacity." - Benjamin Disraeli

I am grateful for...

1. _____
2. _____
3. _____

Daily affirmations. Mind Candy Voice Note *(Record your affirmations on your smart phone and listen to them several times throughout your day)*

I am... _____

_____
_____
_____
_____
_____
_____

My two massive goals to focus on today:

1. _____
2. _____

Take three deep "oxytocin breaths" by placing your hand on your heart and exhaling the sound "haaaaa".

My Mind Candy Minute Journal

Date ____/____/_____

"Teamwork is the long word for success." - Jacquelinemae A. Rudd

I am grateful for...

1. _____
2. _____
3. _____

Daily affirmations. Mind Candy Voice Note *(Record your affirmations on your smart phone and listen to them several times throughout your day)*

I am... _____

_____

_____

_____

_____

_____

_____

My two massive goals to focus on today:

1. _____
2. _____

Take three deep "oxytocin breaths" by placing your hand
on your heart and exhaling the sound "haaaaa".

My Mind Candy Minute Journal

Date ____/____/_____

*"Except and expect positive things and that is
what you will receive." - Lori Hard*

I am grateful for...

1. _____
2. _____
3. _____

Daily affirmations. Mind Candy Voice Note *(Record your affirmations on your smart phone and listen to them several times throughout your day)*

I am... _____

_____
_____
_____
_____
_____
_____

My two massive goals to focus on today:

1. _____
2. _____

Take three deep "oxytocin breaths" by placing your hand
on your heart and exhaling the sound "haaaaa".

My Mind Candy Minute Journal

Date ____/____/_____

"You measure the size of the accomplishment by the obstacles you had to overcome to reach your goals." - Booker T. Washington

I am grateful for...

1. _____
2. _____
3. _____

Daily affirmations. Mind Candy Voice Note *(Record your affirmations on your smart phone and listen to them several times throughout your day)*

I am... _____

_____

_____

_____

_____

_____

_____

My two massive goals to focus on today:

1. _____
2. _____

Take three deep "oxytocin breaths" by placing your hand on your heart and exhaling the sound "haaaaa".

My Mind Candy Minute Journal

Date _____/_____/_____

"In order to succeed you must fail so that you know what not to do the next time." - Anthony J. D'Angelo

I am grateful for...

1. _____
2. _____
3. _____

Daily affirmations. Mind Candy Voice Note *(Record your affirmations on your smart phone and listen to them several times throughout your day)*

I am... _____
_____
_____
_____
_____
_____
_____

My two massive goals to focus on today:

1. _____
2. _____

Take three deep "oxytocin breaths" by placing your hand on your heart and exhaling the sound "haaaaa".

My Mind Candy Minute Journal

Date ____/____/_____

*"Those at the top of the mountain didn't
fall there." - Marcus Washling*

I am grateful for...

1. _____
2. _____
3. _____

Daily affirmations. Mind Candy Voice Note *(Record your affirmations on your smart phone and listen to them several times throughout your day)*

I am... _____

_____
_____
_____
_____
_____
_____

My two massive goals to focus on today:

1. _____
2. _____

Take three deep "oxytocin breaths" by placing your hand
on your heart and exhaling the sound "haaaaa".

My Mind Candy Minute Journal

Date ____/____/_____

"Motivation is what gets you started. Habit is what keeps you going!" - Jim Ryun

I am grateful for...

1. _____
2. _____
3. _____

Daily affirmations. Mind Candy Voice Note *(Record your affirmations on your smart phone and listen to them several times throughout your day)*

I am... _____

_____
_____
_____
_____
_____
_____

My two massive goals to focus on today:

1. _____
2. _____

Take three deep "oxytocin breaths" by placing your hand on your heart and exhaling the sound "haaaaa".

My Mind Candy Minute Journal

Date ____/____/_____

"I am enough of an artist to draw freely upon my imagination. Imagination is more important than knowledge. Knowledge is limited. Imagination encircles the world." - Albert Einstein

I am grateful for...

1. _____
2. _____
3. _____

Daily affirmations. Mind Candy Voice Note *(Record your affirmations on your smart phone and listen to them several times throughout your day)*

I am... _____

_____
_____
_____
_____
_____
_____
_____

My two massive goals to focus on today:

1. _____
2. _____

Take three deep "oxytocin breaths" by placing your hand on your heart and exhaling the sound "haaaaa".

My Mind Candy Minute Journal

Date _____/_____/_____

*"Only those who risk going too far can possibly
find out how far one can go." - T.S. Eliot*

I am grateful for...

1. _____
2. _____
3. _____

Daily affirmations. Mind Candy Voice Note *(Record your affirmations on your smart phone and listen to them several times throughout your day)*

I am... _____

_____

_____

_____

_____

_____

_____

My two massive goals to focus on today:

1. _____
2. _____

Take three deep "oxytocin breaths" by placing your hand
on your heart and exhaling the sound "haaaaa".

My Mind Candy Minute Journal

Date ____/____/_____

"It's amazing what ordinary people can do if they set out without preconceived notions." - Charles F. Kettering

I am grateful for...

1. _____
2. _____
3. _____

Daily affirmations. Mind Candy Voice Note *(Record your affirmations on your smart phone and listen to them several times throughout your day)*

I am... _____

_____
_____
_____
_____
_____
_____

My two massive goals to focus on today:

1. _____
2. _____

Take three deep "oxytocin breaths" by placing your hand on your heart and exhaling the sound "haaaaa".

My Mind Candy Minute Journal

Date ____/____/_____

"People who are afraid to fail can never experience the joys of success." - Pete Zafra

I am grateful for...

1. _____
2. _____
3. _____

Daily affirmations. Mind Candy Voice Note *(Record your affirmations on your smart phone and listen to them several times throughout your day)*

I am... _____

_____
_____
_____
_____
_____
_____

My two massive goals to focus on today:

1. _____
2. _____

Take three deep "oxytocin breaths" by placing your hand on your heart and exhaling the sound "haaaaa".

My Mind Candy Minute Journal

Date ____/____/_____

"No matter how small, acknowledge the achievement." - Greg Henry Quinn

I am grateful for...

1. _____
2. _____
3. _____

Daily affirmations. Mind Candy Voice Note *(Record your affirmations on your smart phone and listen to them several times throughout your day)*

I am... _____

_____
_____
_____
_____
_____
_____

My two massive goals to focus on today:

1. _____
2. _____

Take three deep "oxytocin breaths" by placing your hand on your heart and exhaling the sound "haaaaa".

My Mind Candy Minute Journal

Date ____/____/_____

"If you don't quit, and don't cheat, and don't run home when trouble arrives, you can only win." - Shelley Long

I am grateful for...

1. _____
2. _____
3. _____

Daily affirmations. Mind Candy Voice Note *(Record your affirmations on your smart phone and listen to them several times throughout your day)*

I am... _____
_____
_____
_____
_____
_____
_____

My two massive goals to focus on today:

1. _____
2. _____

Take three deep "oxytocin breaths" by placing your hand on your heart and exhaling the sound "haaaaa".

My Mind Candy Minute Journal

Date ____/____/_____

"Put your heart, mind, intellect, and soul even to your smallest acts. This is the secret of success." - Swami Sivananda

I am grateful for...

1. _____
2. _____
3. _____

Daily affirmations. Mind Candy Voice Note *(Record your affirmations on your smart phone and listen to them several times throughout your day)*

I am... _____

_____
_____
_____
_____
_____
_____

My two massive goals to focus on today:

1. _____
2. _____

Take three deep "oxytocin breaths" by placing your hand on your heart and exhaling the sound "haaaaa".

My Mind Candy Minute Journal

Date ____/____/_____

"The person who makes a success of living is the one who sees his goal steadily and aims for it unswervingly. That is dedication." - Cecil B. DeMille

I am grateful for...

1. _____
2. _____
3. _____

Daily affirmations. Mind Candy Voice Note *(Record your affirmations on your smart phone and listen to them several times throughout your day)*

I am... _____

_____
_____
_____
_____
_____
_____
_____

My two massive goals to focus on today:

1. _____
2. _____

Take three deep "oxytocin breaths" by placing your hand on your heart and exhaling the sound "haaaaa".

My Mind Candy Minute Journal

Date ____/____/_____

"One only gets to the top rung on the ladder by steadily climbing up one at a time, and suddenly, all sorts of powers, all sorts of abilities which you thought never belonged to

I am grateful for...

1. _____
2. _____
3. _____

Daily affirmations. Mind Candy Voice Note *(Record your affirmations on your smart phone and listen to them several times throughout your day)*

I am... _____

_____
_____
_____
_____
_____
_____

My two massive goals to focus on today:

1. _____
2. _____

Take three deep "oxytocin breaths" by placing your hand on your heart and exhaling the sound "haaaaa".

My Mind Candy Minute Journal

Date ____/____/_____

you - suddenly become within your own possibility and you think, 'Well, I'll have a go, too.'" - Margaret Thatcher

I am grateful for...

1. _____
2. _____
3. _____

Daily affirmations. Mind Candy Voice Note *(Record your affirmations on your smart phone and listen to them several times throughout your day)*

I am... _____

_____
_____
_____
_____
_____
_____

My two massive goals to focus on today:

1. _____
2. _____

Take three deep "oxytocin breaths" by placing your hand on your heart and exhaling the sound "haaaaa".

My Mind Candy Minute Journal

Date ____/____/_____

"It is in the small decisions you and I make every day that create our destiny." - Anthony Robbins

I am grateful for...

1. _____
2. _____
3. _____

Daily affirmations. Mind Candy Voice Note *(Record your affirmations on your smart phone and listen to them several times throughout your day)*

I am... _____

_____
_____
_____
_____
_____
_____

My two massive goals to focus on today:

1. _____
2. _____

Take three deep "oxytocin breaths" by placing your hand on your heart and exhaling the sound "haaaaa".

My Mind Candy Minute Journal

Date ____/____/_____

"Deliver more than you are getting paid to do. The victory of success will be half won when you learn the secret of putting out more than is expected in all that you do. Make yourself so valuable in your work that eventually you will become indispensable. Exercise your privilege to go the extra mile, and enjoy all the rewards you receive." - Og Mandino

I am grateful for...

1. _____
2. _____
3. _____

Daily affirmations. Mind Candy Voice Note *(Record your affirmations on your smart phone and listen to them several times throughout your day)*

I am... _____
_____
_____
_____
_____
_____
_____

My two massive goals to focus on today:

1. _____
2. _____

Take three deep "oxytocin breaths" by placing your hand on your heart and exhaling the sound "haaaaa".

My Mind Candy Minute Journal

Date ____/____/_____

"Life is not easy for any of us, but what of that? We must have perseverance and above all confidence in ourselves." - Marie Curie

I am grateful for...

1. _____
2. _____
3. _____

Daily affirmations. Mind Candy Voice Note *(Record your affirmations on your smart phone and listen to them several times throughout your day)*

I am... _____

_____
_____
_____
_____
_____
_____

My two massive goals to focus on today:

1. _____
2. _____

Take three deep "oxytocin breaths" by placing your hand
on your heart and exhaling the sound "haaaaa".

My Mind Candy Minute Journal

Date ____/____/_____

"There are two primary choices in life: to accept conditions as they exist, or accept the responsibility for changing them." - Denis Waitley

I am grateful for...

1. _____
2. _____
3. _____

Daily affirmations. Mind Candy Voice Note *(Record your affirmations on your smart phone and listen to them several times throughout your day)*

I am... _____

_____
_____
_____
_____
_____
_____
_____

My two massive goals to focus on today:

1. _____
2. _____

Take three deep "oxytocin breaths" by placing your hand on your heart and exhaling the sound "haaaaa".

My Mind Candy Minute Journal

Date ____/____/_____

"Effective people are not problem-minded; they're opportunity-minded. They feed opportunities and starve problems." - Stephen Covey

I am grateful for...

1. _____
2. _____
3. _____

Daily affirmations. Mind Candy Voice Note *(Record your affirmations on your smart phone and listen to them several times throughout your day)*

I am... _____

_____
_____
_____
_____
_____
_____

My two massive goals to focus on today:

1. _____
2. _____

Take three deep "oxytocin breaths" by placing your hand on your heart and exhaling the sound "haaaaa".

My Mind Candy Minute Journal

Date ____/____/_____

"A professional is a person who can do his best at a time when he doesn't particularly feel like it." - Alistair Cooke

I am grateful for...

1. _____
2. _____
3. _____

Daily affirmations. Mind Candy Voice Note *(Record your affirmations on your smart phone and listen to them several times throughout your day)*

I am... _____

_____
_____
_____
_____
_____
_____

My two massive goals to focus on today:

1. _____
2. _____

Take three deep "oxytocin breaths" by placing your hand on your heart and exhaling the sound "haaaaa".

My Mind Candy Minute Journal

Date ____/____/_____

"Whatever your grade or position, if you know how and when to speak, and when to remain silent, your chances of real success are proportionately increased." - Ralph C. Smedley

I am grateful for...

1. _____
2. _____
3. _____

Daily affirmations. Mind Candy Voice Note *(Record your affirmations on your smart phone and listen to them several times throughout your day)*

I am... _____

_____
_____
_____
_____
_____
_____

My two massive goals to focus on today:

1. _____
2. _____

Take three deep "oxytocin breaths" by placing your hand on your heart and exhaling the sound "haaaaa".

My Mind Candy Minute Journal

Date ____/____/_____

"I do not think there is any other quality so essential to success of any kind as the quality of perseverance. It overcomes almost everything, even nature." - John D. Rockefeller

I am grateful for...

1. _____
2. _____
3. _____

Daily affirmations. Mind Candy Voice Note *(Record your affirmations on your smart phone and listen to them several times throughout your day)*

I am... _____

_____
_____
_____
_____
_____
_____

My two massive goals to focus on today:

1. _____
2. _____

Take three deep "oxytocin breaths" by placing your hand on your heart and exhaling the sound "haaaaa".

My Mind Candy Minute Journal

Date ____/____/_____

"I know the price of success: dedication, hard work and an unremitting devotion to the things you want to see happen." - Frank Lloyd Wright

I am grateful for...

1. _____
2. _____
3. _____

Daily affirmations. Mind Candy Voice Note *(Record your affirmations on your smart phone and listen to them several times throughout your day)*

I am... _____

_____
_____
_____
_____
_____
_____

My two massive goals to focus on today:

1. _____
2. _____

Take three deep "oxytocin breaths" by placing your hand on your heart and exhaling the sound "haaaaa".

My Mind Candy Minute Journal

Date _____/_____/_____

"Do not fear to be eccentric in opinion, for every opinion now accepted was once eccentric." - Bertrand Russell

I am grateful for...

1. _____
2. _____
3. _____

Daily affirmations. Mind Candy Voice Note *(Record your affirmations on your smart phone and listen to them several times throughout your day)*

I am... _____

_____
_____
_____
_____
_____
_____

My two massive goals to focus on today:

1. _____
2. _____

Take three deep "oxytocin breaths" by placing your hand on your heart and exhaling the sound "haaaaa".

My Mind Candy Minute Journal

Date ____/____/_____

"Each problem has hidden in it an opportunity so powerful that it literally dwarfs the problem. The greatest success stories were created by people who recognized a problem and turned it into an opportunity." - Joseph Sugarman

I am grateful for...

1. _____
2. _____
3. _____

Daily affirmations. Mind Candy Voice Note *(Record your affirmations on your smart phone and listen to them several times throughout your day)*

I am... _____

_____
_____
_____
_____
_____
_____
_____

My two massive goals to focus on today:

1. _____
2. _____

Take three deep "oxytocin breaths" by placing your hand on your heart and exhaling the sound "haaaaa".

My Mind Candy Minute Journal

Date ____/____/_____

"Fortunate is the person who has developed the self-control to steer a straight course towards his objective in life, without being swayed from his purpose by either commendation or condemnation." - Napoleon Hill

I am grateful for...

1. _____
2. _____
3. _____

Daily affirmations. Mind Candy Voice Note *(Record your affirmations on your smart phone and listen to them several times throughout your day)*

I am... _____
_____
_____
_____
_____
_____
_____

My two massive goals to focus on today:

1. _____
2. _____

Take three deep "oxytocin breaths" by placing your hand on your heart and exhaling the sound "haaaaa".

My Mind Candy Minute Journal

Date ____/____/_____

"Never let your work drive you. Master it and keep it in complete control." - Booker T. Washington

I am grateful for...

1. _____
2. _____
3. _____

Daily affirmations. Mind Candy Voice Note *(Record your affirmations on your smart phone and listen to them several times throughout your day)*

I am... _____

_____
_____
_____
_____
_____
_____

My two massive goals to focus on today:

1. _____
2. _____

Take three deep "oxytocin breaths" by placing your hand on your heart and exhaling the sound "haaaaa".

My Mind Candy Minute Journal

Date ____/____/_____

"Follow your dream as long as you live, do not lessen the time of following desire, for wasting time is an abomination of the spirit." - Plato

I am grateful for...

1. _____
2. _____
3. _____

Daily affirmations. Mind Candy Voice Note *(Record your affirmations on your smart phone and listen to them several times throughout your day)*

I am... _____

_____

_____

_____

_____

_____

_____

My two massive goals to focus on today:

1. _____
2. _____

Take three deep "oxytocin breaths" by placing your hand on your heart and exhaling the sound "haaaaa".

My Mind Candy Minute Journal

Date ____/____/_____

"You say I started out with practically nothing, but that isn't correct. We all start with all there is. It's how we use it that makes things possible." - Henry Ford

I am grateful for...

1. _____
2. _____
3. _____

Daily affirmations. Mind Candy Voice Note *(Record your affirmations on your smart phone and listen to them several times throughout your day)*

I am... _____

_____
_____
_____
_____
_____
_____

My two massive goals to focus on today:

1. _____
2. _____

Take three deep "oxytocin breaths" by placing your hand on your heart and exhaling the sound "haaaaa".

My Mind Candy Minute Journal

Date ____/____/_____

"I don't have to be what nobody else wants me to be and I am not afraid to be what I want to be." - Muhammad Ali

I am grateful for...

1. _____
2. _____
3. _____

Daily affirmations. Mind Candy Voice Note *(Record your affirmations on your smart phone and listen to them several times throughout your day)*

I am... _____

_____
_____
_____
_____
_____
_____

My two massive goals to focus on today:

1. _____
2. _____

Take three deep "oxytocin breaths" by placing your hand on your heart and exhaling the sound "haaaaa".

My Mind Candy Minute Journal

Date _____/_____/_____

"The highest reward for one's toil is not what one gets for it, but what one becomes by it." - John Ruskin

I am grateful for...

1. _____
2. _____
3. _____

Daily affirmations. Mind Candy Voice Note *(Record your affirmations on your smart phone and listen to them several times throughout your day)*

I am... _____

_____
_____
_____
_____
_____
_____

My two massive goals to focus on today:

1. _____
2. _____

Take three deep "oxytocin breaths" by placing your hand on your heart and exhaling the sound "haaaaa".

My Mind Candy Minute Journal

Date ____/____/_____

"I studied the lives of great men and women, and I found that the men and women who got to the top were those who did the jobs they had in hand, with everything they had of energy and enthusiasm and hard work." - Harry S. Truman

I am grateful for...

1. _____
2. _____
3. _____

Daily affirmations. Mind Candy Voice Note *(Record your affirmations on your smart phone and listen to them several times throughout your day)*

I am... _____

_____
_____
_____
_____
_____
_____

My two massive goals to focus on today:

1. _____
2. _____

Take three deep "oxytocin breaths" by placing your hand on your heart and exhaling the sound "haaaaa".

My Mind Candy Minute Journal

Date ____/____/_____

"The seat of freedom is reserved for the man who lives by his own work, and in that work, does what he wants to do." - George Robin Collingwood

I am grateful for...

1. _____
2. _____
3. _____

Daily affirmations. Mind Candy Voice Note *(Record your affirmations on your smart phone and listen to them several times throughout your day)*

I am... _____

_____
_____
_____
_____
_____
_____

My two massive goals to focus on today:

1. _____
2. _____

Take three deep "oxytocin breaths" by placing your hand on your heart and exhaling the sound "haaaaa".

My Mind Candy Minute Journal

Date ____/____/_____

"Success is measured in terms of reaching your goals, dreams, and expectations. Your success is determined by hard work, persistence, and determination. If you are going to be a success in life, it is up to you... it is your responsibility." - Will Horton

I am grateful for...

1. _____
2. _____
3. _____

Daily affirmations. Mind Candy Voice Note *(Record your affirmations on your smart phone and listen to them several times throughout your day)*

I am... _____

_____
_____
_____
_____
_____
_____

My two massive goals to focus on today:

1. _____
2. _____

Take three deep "oxytocin breaths" by placing your hand on your heart and exhaling the sound "haaaaa".

My Mind Candy Minute Journal

Date ____/____/_____

"The difference between success and mediocrity is all in the way you think." - Dean Francis

I am grateful for...

1. _____
2. _____
3. _____

Daily affirmations. Mind Candy Voice Note *(Record your affirmations on your smart phone and listen to them several times throughout your day)*

I am... _____

_____
_____
_____
_____
_____
_____
_____

My two massive goals to focus on today:

1. _____
2. _____

Take three deep "oxytocin breaths" by placing your hand on your heart and exhaling the sound "haaaaa".

My Mind Candy Minute Journal

Date ____/____/_____

"You are never too old to set another goal or to dream a new dream." - Les Brown

I am grateful for...

1. _____
2. _____
3. _____

Daily affirmations. Mind Candy Voice Note *(Record your affirmations on your smart phone and listen to them several times throughout your day)*

I am... _____

_____
_____
_____
_____
_____
_____

My two massive goals to focus on today:

1. _____
2. _____

Take three deep "oxytocin breaths" by placing your hand on your heart and exhaling the sound "haaaaa".

My Mind Candy Minute Journal

Date ____/____/_____

"What separates those who achieve from those who do not is in direct proportion to one's ability to ask for help." - Donald Keough

I am grateful for...

1. _____
2. _____
3. _____

Daily affirmations. Mind Candy Voice Note *(Record your affirmations on your smart phone and listen to them several times throughout your day)*

I am... _____

_____

_____

_____

_____

_____

My two massive goals to focus on today:

1. _____
2. _____

Take three deep "oxytocin breaths" by placing your hand on your heart and exhaling the sound "haaaaa".

My Mind Candy Minute Journal

Date ____/____/_____

"You only have to do a very few things right in your life so long as you don't do too many things wrong." - Warren Buffett

I am grateful for...

1. _____
2. _____
3. _____

Daily affirmations. Mind Candy Voice Note *(Record your affirmations on your smart phone and listen to them several times throughout your day)*

I am... _____
_____
_____
_____
_____
_____
_____

My two massive goals to focus on today:

1. _____
2. _____

Take three deep "oxytocin breaths" by placing your hand on your heart and exhaling the sound "haaaaa".

My Mind Candy Minute Journal

Date ____/____/_____

*"It is wise to keep in mind that neither success
nor failure is ever final." - Roger Babson*

I am grateful for...

1. _____
2. _____
3. _____

Daily affirmations. Mind Candy Voice Note *(Record your affirmations on your smart phone and listen to them several times throughout your day)*

I am... _____

_____
_____
_____
_____
_____
_____

My two massive goals to focus on today:

1. _____
2. _____

Take three deep "oxytocin breaths" by placing your hand
on your heart and exhaling the sound "haaaaa".

My Mind Candy Minute Journal

Date ____/____/_____

"Success is a journey, not a destination." - Ben Sweetland

I am grateful for...

1. _____
2. _____
3. _____

Daily affirmations. Mind Candy Voice Note *(Record your affirmations on your smart phone and listen to them several times throughout your day)*

I am... _____

_____

_____

_____

_____

_____

_____

My two massive goals to focus on today:

1. _____
2. _____

Take three deep "oxytocin breaths" by placing your hand
on your heart and exhaling the sound "haaaaa".

My Mind Candy Minute Journal

Date ____/____/_____

"To guarantee success, act as if it were impossible to fail." - Dorothea Brande

I am grateful for...

1. _____
2. _____
3. _____

Daily affirmations. Mind Candy Voice Note *(Record your affirmations on your smart phone and listen to them several times throughout your day)*

I am... _____

_____
_____
_____
_____
_____
_____

My two massive goals to focus on today:

1. _____
2. _____

Take three deep "oxytocin breaths" by placing your hand on your heart and exhaling the sound "haaaaa".

My Mind Candy Minute Journal

Date _____/_____/_____

"Success is often the result of taking a misstep in the right direction." - Al Bernstein

I am grateful for...

1. _____
2. _____
3. _____

Daily affirmations. Mind Candy Voice Note *(Record your affirmations on your smart phone and listen to them several times throughout your day)*

I am... _____

_____
_____
_____
_____
_____
_____

My two massive goals to focus on today:

1. _____
2. _____

Take three deep "oxytocin breaths" by placing your hand on your heart and exhaling the sound "haaaaa".

My Mind Candy Minute Journal

Date ____/____/_____

"You can do it if you believe you can." - Napoleon Hill

I am grateful for...

1. _____
2. _____
3. _____

Daily affirmations. Mind Candy Voice Note *(Record your affirmations on your smart phone and listen to them several times throughout your day)*

I am... _____

_____
_____
_____
_____
_____
_____

My two massive goals to focus on today:

1. _____
2. _____

Take three deep "oxytocin breaths" by placing your hand on your heart and exhaling the sound "haaaaa".

My Mind Candy Minute Journal

Date ____/____/_____

"Success is simply a matter of luck. Ask any failure." - Earl Wilson

I am grateful for...

1. _____
2. _____
3. _____

Daily affirmations. Mind Candy Voice Note *(Record your affirmations on your smart phone and listen to them several times throughout your day)*

I am... _____
_____
_____
_____
_____
_____
_____

My two massive goals to focus on today:

1. _____
2. _____

Take three deep "oxytocin breaths" by placing your hand on your heart and exhaling the sound "haaaaa".

My Mind Candy Minute Journal

Date ____/____/_____

"I like a state of continual becoming, with a goal in front and not behind." - George Bernard Shaw

I am grateful for...

1. _____
2. _____
3. _____

Daily affirmations. Mind Candy Voice Note *(Record your affirmations on your smart phone and listen to them several times throughout your day)*

I am... _____

_____

_____

_____

_____

_____

My two massive goals to focus on today:

1. _____
2. _____

Take three deep "oxytocin breaths" by placing your hand on your heart and exhaling the sound "haaaaa".

My Mind Candy Minute Journal

Date ____/____/_____

"You must do the very thing you think you cannot do." - Eleanor Roosevelt

I am grateful for...

1. _____
2. _____
3. _____

Daily affirmations. Mind Candy Voice Note *(Record your affirmations on your smart phone and listen to them several times throughout your day)*

I am... _____

_____
_____
_____
_____
_____
_____

My two massive goals to focus on today:

1. _____
2. _____

Take three deep "oxytocin breaths" by placing your hand on your heart and exhaling the sound "haaaaa".

My Mind Candy Minute Journal

Date ____/____/_____

"Flaming enthusiasm, backed by horse-sense and persistence, is the quality that most frequently makes for success." - Dale Carnegie

I am grateful for...

1. _____
2. _____
3. _____

Daily affirmations. Mind Candy Voice Note *(Record your affirmations on your smart phone and listen to them several times throughout your day)*

I am... _____

_____
_____
_____
_____
_____
_____

My two massive goals to focus on today:

1. _____
2. _____

Take three deep "oxytocin breaths" by placing your hand on your heart and exhaling the sound "haaaaa".

My Mind Candy Minute Journal

Date ____/____/_____

"It's the repetition of affirmations that leads to belief. And once that belief becomes a deep conviction, things begin to happen." - Claude M. Bristol

I am grateful for...

1. _____
2. _____
3. _____

Daily affirmations. Mind Candy Voice Note *(Record your affirmations on your smart phone and listen to them several times throughout your day)*

I am... _____

_____
_____
_____
_____
_____
_____

My two massive goals to focus on today:

1. _____
2. _____

Take three deep "oxytocin breaths" by placing your hand on your heart and exhaling the sound "haaaaa".

My Mind Candy Minute Journal

Date ____/____/_____

"The biggest temptation is to settle for too little." - Thomas Merton

I am grateful for...

1. _____
2. _____
3. _____

Daily affirmations. Mind Candy Voice Note *(Record your affirmations on your smart phone and listen to them several times throughout your day)*

I am... _____

_____
_____
_____
_____
_____
_____

My two massive goals to focus on today:

1. _____
2. _____

Take three deep "oxytocin breaths" by placing your hand on your heart and exhaling the sound "haaaaa".

My Mind Candy Minute Journal

Date _____/_____/_____

"Yes, I am a dreamer. For a dreamer is one who can find his way by moonlight, and see the dawn before the rest of the world." - Oscar Wilde

I am grateful for...

1. _____
2. _____
3. _____

Daily affirmations. Mind Candy Voice Note *(Record your affirmations on your smart phone and listen to them several times throughout your day)*

I am... _____

_____
_____
_____
_____
_____
_____

My two massive goals to focus on today:

1. _____
2. _____

Take three deep "oxytocin breaths" by placing your hand on your heart and exhaling the sound "haaaaa".

My Mind Candy Minute Journal

Date ____/____/_____

"Don't dream it. Be it!" - Richard O'brian

I am grateful for...

1. _____
2. _____
3. _____

Daily affirmations. Mind Candy Voice Note *(Record your affirmations on your smart phone and listen to them several times throughout your day)*

I am... _____

_____

_____

_____

_____

_____

_____

My two massive goals to focus on today:

1. _____
2. _____

Take three deep "oxytocin breaths" by placing your hand on your heart and exhaling the sound "haaaaa".

My Mind Candy Minute Journal

Date ____/____/_____

"He has achieved success who has lived well, laughed often and loved much." - Bessie Anderson Stanley

I am grateful for...

1. _____
2. _____
3. _____

Daily affirmations. Mind Candy Voice Note *(Record your affirmations on your smart phone and listen to them several times throughout your day)*

I am... _____

_____

_____

_____

_____

_____

_____

My two massive goals to focus on today:

1. _____
2. _____

Take three deep "oxytocin breaths" by placing your hand on your heart and exhaling the sound "haaaaa".

My Mind Candy Minute Journal

Date ____/____/_____

"If you don't go after what you want, you'll never have it. If you don't ask, the answer is always no. If you don't step forward, you're always in the same place." - Nora Roberts

I am grateful for...

1. _____
2. _____
3. _____

Daily affirmations. Mind Candy Voice Note *(Record your affirmations on your smart phone and listen to them several times throughout your day)*

I am... _____

_____
_____
_____
_____
_____
_____
_____

My two massive goals to focus on today:

1. _____
2. _____

Take three deep "oxytocin breaths" by placing your hand on your heart and exhaling the sound "haaaaa".

My Mind Candy Minute Journal

Date ____/____/_____

"Henry Ford could get anything out of men because he just talked and would tell them stories. He'd never say, 'I want this done!' He'd say, 'I wonder if we can do it.'" - George Brown

I am grateful for...

1. _____
2. _____
3. _____

Daily affirmations. Mind Candy Voice Note *(Record your affirmations on your smart phone and listen to them several times throughout your day)*

I am... _____

_____
_____
_____
_____
_____
_____

My two massive goals to focus on today:

1. _____
2. _____

Take three deep "oxytocin breaths" by placing your hand on your heart and exhaling the sound "haaaaa".

My Mind Candy Minute Journal

Date ____/____/_____

"Those who dream by day are cognizant of many things which escape those who dream only by night." - Edgar Allen Poe

I am grateful for...

1. _____
2. _____
3. _____

Daily affirmations. Mind Candy Voice Note *(Record your affirmations on your smart phone and listen to them several times throughout your day)*

I am... _____

_____
_____
_____
_____
_____

My two massive goals to focus on today:

1. _____
2. _____

Take three deep "oxytocin breaths" by placing your hand on your heart and exhaling the sound "haaaaa".

My Mind Candy Minute Journal

Date ____/____/_____

"The key to happiness is having dreams; the key to success is making them come true." - James Allen

I am grateful for...

1. _____
2. _____
3. _____

Daily affirmations. Mind Candy Voice Note *(Record your affirmations on your smart phone and listen to them several times throughout your day)*

I am... _____

_____
_____
_____
_____
_____
_____

My two massive goals to focus on today:

1. _____
2. _____

Take three deep "oxytocin breaths" by placing your hand on your heart and exhaling the sound "haaaaa".

My Mind Candy Minute Journal

Date ____/____/_____

"Life is a series of problem-solving opportunities. The problems you face will either defeat you or develop you depending on how you respond to them." - Rick Warren

I am grateful for...

1. _____
2. _____
3. _____

Daily affirmations. Mind Candy Voice Note *(Record your affirmations on your smart phone and listen to them several times throughout your day)*

I am... _____

_____
_____
_____
_____
_____
_____
_____

My two massive goals to focus on today:

1. _____
2. _____

Take three deep "oxytocin breaths" by placing your hand on your heart and exhaling the sound "haaaaa".

My Mind Candy Minute Journal

Date ____/____/_____

"All men who have achieved great things have been great dreamers." - Orison Swett Marden

I am grateful for...

1. _____
2. _____
3. _____

Daily affirmations. Mind Candy Voice Note *(Record your affirmations on your smart phone and listen to them several times throughout your day)*

I am... _____
_____
_____
_____
_____
_____
_____

My two massive goals to focus on today:

1. _____
2. _____

Take three deep "oxytocin breaths" by placing your hand on your heart and exhaling the sound "haaaaa".

My Mind Candy Minute Journal

Date ____/____/_____

"Success is doing ordinary things extraordinarily well." - Jim Rohn

I am grateful for...

1. _____
2. _____
3. _____

Daily affirmations. Mind Candy Voice Note *(Record your affirmations on your smart phone and listen to them several times throughout your day)*

I am... _____

_____

_____

_____

_____

_____

_____

My two massive goals to focus on today:

1. _____
2. _____

Take three deep "oxytocin breaths" by placing your hand on your heart and exhaling the sound "haaaaa".

My Mind Candy Minute Journal

Date ____/____/_____

"I start with the premise that the function of leadership is to produce more leaders, not more followers." - Ralph Nader

I am grateful for...

1. _____
2. _____
3. _____

Daily affirmations. Mind Candy Voice Note *(Record your affirmations on your smart phone and listen to them several times throughout your day)*

I am... _____

_____
_____
_____
_____
_____
_____

My two massive goals to focus on today:

1. _____
2. _____

Take three deep "oxytocin breaths" by placing your hand on your heart and exhaling the sound "haaaaa".

My Mind Candy Minute Journal

Date ____/____/_____

"Never walk away from failure. On the contrary, study it carefully and imaginatively for its hidden assets." - Michael Korda

I am grateful for...

1. _____
2. _____
3. _____

Daily affirmations. Mind Candy Voice Note *(Record your affirmations on your smart phone and listen to them several times throughout your day)*

I am... _____

_____
_____
_____
_____
_____

My two massive goals to focus on today:

1. _____
2. _____

Take three deep "oxytocin breaths" by placing your hand on your heart and exhaling the sound "haaaaa".

My Mind Candy Minute Journal

Date ____/____/_____

"Nothing ever comes to one that is worth having except as a result of hard work." - Booker T. Washington

I am grateful for...

1. _____
2. _____
3. _____

Daily affirmations. Mind Candy Voice Note *(Record your affirmations on your smart phone and listen to them several times throughout your day)*

I am... _____

_____
_____
_____
_____
_____
_____

My two massive goals to focus on today:

1. _____
2. _____

Take three deep "oxytocin breaths" by placing your hand on your heart and exhaling the sound "haaaaa".

My Mind Candy Minute Journal

Date ____/____/_____

"You cannot control what happens to you, but you can control your attitude toward what happens to you, and in that, you will be mastering change rather than allowing it to master you." - Brian Tracy

I am grateful for...

1. _____
2. _____
3. _____

Daily affirmations. Mind Candy Voice Note *(Record your affirmations on your smart phone and listen to them several times throughout your day)*

I am... _____
_____
_____
_____
_____
_____
_____

My two massive goals to focus on today:

1. _____
2. _____

Take three deep "oxytocin breaths" by placing your hand on your heart and exhaling the sound "haaaaa".

My Mind Candy Minute Journal

Date ____/____/_____

"I learned that the only way you are going to get anywhere in life is to work hard at it. Whether you're a musician, a writer, an athlete or a businessman, there is no getting around it. If you do, you'll win - if you don't you won't." - Bruce Jenner

I am grateful for...

1. _____
2. _____
3. _____

Daily affirmations. Mind Candy Voice Note *(Record your affirmations on your smart phone and listen to them several times throughout your day)*

I am... _____

_____
_____
_____
_____
_____
_____
_____

My two massive goals to focus on today:

1. _____
2. _____

Take three deep "oxytocin breaths" by placing your hand on your heart and exhaling the sound "haaaaa".

My Mind Candy Minute Journal

Date ____/____/_____

"Unless you are willing to drench yourself in your work beyond the capacity of the average man, you are just not cut out for positions at the top." - J.C. Penny

I am grateful for...

1. _____
2. _____
3. _____

Daily affirmations. Mind Candy Voice Note *(Record your affirmations on your smart phone and listen to them several times throughout your day)*

I am... _____

_____
_____
_____
_____
_____
_____

My two massive goals to focus on today:

1. _____
2. _____

Take three deep "oxytocin breaths" by placing your hand on your heart and exhaling the sound "haaaaa".

My Mind Candy Minute Journal

Date ____/____/_____

"Success is not measured by what a man accomplishes, but by the opposition he has encountered and the courage with which he has maintained the struggle against overwhelming odds." - Charles Lindbergh

I am grateful for...

1. _____
2. _____
3. _____

Daily affirmations. Mind Candy Voice Note *(Record your affirmations on your smart phone and listen to them several times throughout your day)*

I am... _____

_____
_____
_____
_____
_____
_____

My two massive goals to focus on today:

1. _____
2. _____

Take three deep "oxytocin breaths" by placing your hand on your heart and exhaling the sound "haaaaa".

My Mind Candy Minute Journal

Date ____/____/_____

"If you have the will to win, you have achieved half your success; if you don't, you have achieved half your failure." - David Ambrose

I am grateful for...

1. _____
2. _____
3. _____

Daily affirmations. Mind Candy Voice Note *(Record your affirmations on your smart phone and listen to them several times throughout your day)*

I am... _____

_____
_____
_____
_____
_____
_____

My two massive goals to focus on today:

1. _____
2. _____

Take three deep "oxytocin breaths" by placing your hand on your heart and exhaling the sound "haaaaa".

My Mind Candy Minute Journal

Date ____/____/_____

"You may be disappointed if you fail, but you are doomed if you don't try." - Beverly Sills

I am grateful for...

1. _____
2. _____
3. _____

Daily affirmations. Mind Candy Voice Note *(Record your affirmations on your smart phone and listen to them several times throughout your day)*

I am... _____

_____
_____
_____
_____
_____
_____

My two massive goals to focus on today:

1. _____
2. _____

Take three deep "oxytocin breaths" by placing your hand on your heart and exhaling the sound "haaaaa".

My Mind Candy Minute Journal

Date ____/____/_____

"Unless you try to do something beyond what you have already mastered, you will never grow." - Ronald E. Osborn

I am grateful for...

1. _____
2. _____
3. _____

Daily affirmations. Mind Candy Voice Note *(Record your affirmations on your smart phone and listen to them several times throughout your day)*

I am... _____
_____
_____
_____
_____
_____

My two massive goals to focus on today:

1. _____
2. _____

Take three deep "oxytocin breaths" by placing your hand on your heart and exhaling the sound "haaaaa".

My Mind Candy Minute Journal

Date ____/____/_____

"Your success and happiness lie in you." - Helen Keller

I am grateful for...

1. _____
2. _____
3. _____

Daily affirmations. Mind Candy Voice Note *(Record your affirmations on your smart phone and listen to them several times throughout your day)*

I am... _____

_____
_____
_____
_____
_____
_____

My two massive goals to focus on today:

1. _____
2. _____

Take three deep "oxytocin breaths" by placing your hand on your heart and exhaling the sound "haaaaa".

My Mind Candy Minute Journal

Date ____/____/_____

"Successful and unsuccessful people do not vary greatly in their abilities. They vary in their desires to reach their potential." - John Maxwell

I am grateful for...

1. _____
2. _____
3. _____

Daily affirmations. Mind Candy Voice Note *(Record your affirmations on your smart phone and listen to them several times throughout your day)*

I am... _____

_____

_____

_____

_____

_____

_____

My two massive goals to focus on today:

1. _____
2. _____

Take three deep "oxytocin breaths" by placing your hand on your heart and exhaling the sound "haaaaa".

My Mind Candy Minute Journal

Date ____/____/_____

"The only difference between a success and a failure is that the successful person is willing to do what the failure is not willing to do." - J.R. Ridinger

I am grateful for...

1. _____
2. _____
3. _____

Daily affirmations. Mind Candy Voice Note *(Record your affirmations on your smart phone and listen to them several times throughout your day)*

I am... _____

_____
_____
_____
_____
_____
_____

My two massive goals to focus on today:

1. _____
2. _____

Take three deep "oxytocin breaths" by placing your hand on your heart and exhaling the sound "haaaaa".

My Mind Candy Minute Journal

Date ____/____/_____

"The man who moved a mountain was the one who began carrying away small stones." - Chinese Proverb

I am grateful for...

1. _____
2. _____
3. _____

Daily affirmations. Mind Candy Voice Note *(Record your affirmations on your smart phone and listen to them several times throughout your day)*

I am... _____

_____
_____
_____
_____
_____
_____

My two massive goals to focus on today:

1. _____
2. _____

Take three deep "oxytocin breaths" by placing your hand on your heart and exhaling the sound "haaaaa".

My Mind Candy Minute Journal

Date ____/____/_____

"Winning isn't everything. It's the only thing." - Vincent Lombardi

I am grateful for...

1. _____
2. _____
3. _____

Daily affirmations. Mind Candy Voice Note *(Record your affirmations on your smart phone and listen to them several times throughout your day)*

I am... _____

_____

_____

_____

_____

_____

My two massive goals to focus on today:

1. _____
2. _____

Take three deep "oxytocin breaths" by placing your hand on your heart and exhaling the sound "haaaaa".

My Mind Candy Minute Journal

Date ____/____/_____

"Your imagination is your preview of life's coming attractions." - Albert Einstein

I am grateful for...

1. _____
2. _____
3. _____

Daily affirmations. Mind Candy Voice Note *(Record your affirmations on your smart phone and listen to them several times throughout your day)*

I am... _____

_____

_____

_____

_____

_____

_____

My two massive goals to focus on today:

1. _____
2. _____

Take three deep "oxytocin breaths" by placing your hand on your heart and exhaling the sound "haaaaa".

My Mind Candy Minute Journal

Date ____/____/_____

"Whatever you do, you need courage. Whatever course you decide upon, there is always someone to tell you that you are wrong. There are always difficulties arising that tempt you to believe your critics are right. To map out a course of action and follow it to an end requires some of the same courage that a soldier needs. Peace has its victories, but it takes brave men and women to win them." - Ralph Waldo Emerson

I am grateful for...

1. _____
2. _____
3. _____

Daily affirmations. Mind Candy Voice Note (*Record your affirmations on your smart phone and listen to them several times throughout your day*)

I am... _____

_____
_____
_____
_____
_____
_____

My two massive goals to focus on today:

1. _____
2. _____

Take three deep "oxytocin breaths" by placing your hand on your heart and exhaling the sound "haaaaa".

My Mind Candy Minute Journal

Date ____/____/_____

"Successful leaders recognize that great innovation comes from observing the same ideas as everyone else and seeing something different." - Reed Markham

I am grateful for...

1. _____
2. _____
3. _____

Daily affirmations. Mind Candy Voice Note *(Record your affirmations on your smart phone and listen to them several times throughout your day)*

I am... _____

_____
_____
_____
_____
_____
_____

My two massive goals to focus on today:

1. _____
2. _____

Take three deep "oxytocin breaths" by placing your hand on your heart and exhaling the sound "haaaaa".

My Mind Candy Minute Journal

Date _____/_____/_____

"Action is the foundational key to all success." - Anthony Robbins

I am grateful for...

1. _____
2. _____
3. _____

Daily affirmations. Mind Candy Voice Note *(Record your affirmations on your smart phone and listen to them several times throughout your day)*

I am... _____

_____
_____
_____
_____
_____
_____

My two massive goals to focus on today:

1. _____
2. _____

Take three deep "oxytocin breaths" by placing your hand on your heart and exhaling the sound "haaaaa".

My Mind Candy Minute Journal

Date ____/____/_____

"Be humble always and identify with the common man; even when success and achievements want to make you proud." - Bishop Leonard Umunna

I am grateful for...

1. _____
2. _____
3. _____

Daily affirmations. Mind Candy Voice Note *(Record your affirmations on your smart phone and listen to them several times throughout your day)*

I am... _____

_____

_____

_____

_____

_____

_____

My two massive goals to focus on today:

1. _____
2. _____

Take three deep "oxytocin breaths" by placing your hand on your heart and exhaling the sound "haaaaa".

My Mind Candy Minute Journal

Date ____/____/_____

"The successful man will profit from his mistakes and try again in a different way." - Dale Carnegie

I am grateful for...

1. _____
2. _____
3. _____

Daily affirmations. Mind Candy Voice Note *(Record your affirmations on your smart phone and listen to them several times throughout your day)*

I am... _____

_____
_____
_____
_____
_____
_____

My two massive goals to focus on today:

1. _____
2. _____

Take three deep "oxytocin breaths" by placing your hand on your heart and exhaling the sound "haaaaa".

My Mind Candy Minute Journal

Date ____/____/_____

"Believe it can be done. When you believe something can be done, really believe, your mind will find the ways to do it. Believing there is a solution paves the way to a solution." - Dr. David Schwartz

I am grateful for...

1. _____
2. _____
3. _____

Daily affirmations. Mind Candy Voice Note *(Record your affirmations on your smart phone and listen to them several times throughout your day)*

I am... _____

_____
_____
_____
_____
_____
_____

My two massive goals to focus on today:

1. _____
2. _____

Take three deep "oxytocin breaths" by placing your hand on your heart and exhaling the sound "haaaaa".

My Mind Candy Minute Journal

Date ____/____/_____

"All successful men and women are big dreamers. They imagine what their future could be, ideal in every respect, and then they work every day toward their distant vision, that goal or purpose." - Brian Tracy

I am grateful for...

1. _____
2. _____
3. _____

Daily affirmations. Mind Candy Voice Note *(Record your affirmations on your smart phone and listen to them several times throughout your day)*

I am... _____

_____
_____
_____
_____
_____
_____

My two massive goals to focus on today:

1. _____
2. _____

Take three deep "oxytocin breaths" by placing your hand on your heart and exhaling the sound "haaaaa".

My Mind Candy Minute Journal

Date ____/____/_____

"The secret of success is to be ready when your opportunity comes." - Benjamin Disraeli

I am grateful for...

1. _____
2. _____
3. _____

Daily affirmations. Mind Candy Voice Note *(Record your affirmations on your smart phone and listen to them several times throughout your day)*

I am... _____

_____
_____
_____
_____
_____
_____

My two massive goals to focus on today:

1. _____
2. _____

Take three deep "oxytocin breaths" by placing your hand on your heart and exhaling the sound "haaaaa".

My Mind Candy Minute Journal

Date ____/____/_____

"We must never be afraid to go too far, for success lies just beyond." - Marcel Proust

I am grateful for...

1. _____
2. _____
3. _____

Daily affirmations. Mind Candy Voice Note *(Record your affirmations on your smart phone and listen to them several times throughout your day)*

I am... _____

_____
_____
_____
_____
_____
_____

My two massive goals to focus on today:

1. _____
2. _____

Take three deep "oxytocin breaths" by placing your hand on your heart and exhaling the sound "haaaaa".

My Mind Candy Minute Journal

Date ____/____/_____

"No one ever attains very eminent success by simply doing what is required of him; it is the amount and excellence of what is over and above the required that determines the greatness of ultimate distinction." - Charles Kendall Adams

I am grateful for...

1. _____
2. _____
3. _____

Daily affirmations. Mind Candy Voice Note *(Record your affirmations on your smart phone and listen to them several times throughout your day)*

I am... _____

_____
_____
_____
_____
_____
_____

My two massive goals to focus on today:

1. _____
2. _____

Take three deep "oxytocin breaths" by placing your hand on your heart and exhaling the sound "haaaaa".

My Mind Candy Minute Journal

Date ____/____/_____

"I will speak ill of no one and speak all the good I know of everybody." - Andrew Jackson

I am grateful for...

1. _____
2. _____
3. _____

Daily affirmations. Mind Candy Voice Note *(Record your affirmations on your smart phone and listen to them several times throughout your day)*

I am... _____

_____
_____
_____
_____
_____
_____

My two massive goals to focus on today:

1. _____
2. _____

Take three deep "oxytocin breaths" by placing your hand on your heart and exhaling the sound "haaaaa".

My Mind Candy Minute Journal

Date ____/____/_____

"You don't become enormously successful without encountering some really interesting problems." - Mark Victor Hansen

I am grateful for...

1. _____
2. _____
3. _____

Daily affirmations. Mind Candy Voice Note *(Record your affirmations on your smart phone and listen to them several times throughout your day)*

I am... _____

_____

_____

_____

_____

_____

_____

My two massive goals to focus on today:

1. _____
2. _____

Take three deep "oxytocin breaths" by placing your hand on your heart and exhaling the sound "haaaaa".

My Mind Candy Minute Journal

Date _____/_____/_____

"I've always tried to go one step past wherever people expected me to end up." - Beverly Sills

I am grateful for...

1. _____
2. _____
3. _____

Daily affirmations. Mind Candy Voice Note *(Record your affirmations on your smart phone and listen to them several times throughout your day)*

I am... _____
_____
_____
_____
_____
_____
_____

My two massive goals to focus on today:

1. _____
2. _____

Take three deep "oxytocin breaths" by placing your hand on your heart and exhaling the sound "haaaaa".

My Mind Candy Minute Journal

Date ____/____/_____

"Few things help an individual more than to place responsibility upon him, and to let him know that you trust him." - Booker T. Washington

I am grateful for...

1. _____
2. _____
3. _____

Daily affirmations. Mind Candy Voice Note *(Record your affirmations on your smart phone and listen to them several times throughout your day)*

I am... _____
_____
_____
_____
_____
_____
_____

My two massive goals to focus on today:

1. _____
2. _____

Take three deep "oxytocin breaths" by placing your hand on your heart and exhaling the sound "haaaaa".

My Mind Candy Minute Journal

Date ____/____/_____

"Don't let the fear of striking out hold you back." - Babe Ruth

I am grateful for...

1. _____
2. _____
3. _____

Daily affirmations. Mind Candy Voice Note *(Record your affirmations on your smart phone and listen to them several times throughout your day)*

I am... _____

_____
_____
_____
_____
_____
_____

My two massive goals to focus on today:

1. _____
2. _____

Take three deep "oxytocin breaths" by placing your hand on your heart and exhaling the sound "haaaaa".

My Mind Candy Minute Journal

Date ____/____/_____

"You have to accept whatever comes and the only important thing is that you meet it with the best you have to give." - Eleanor Roosevelt

I am grateful for...

1. _____
2. _____
3. _____

Daily affirmations. Mind Candy Voice Note *(Record your affirmations on your smart phone and listen to them several times throughout your day)*

I am... _____
_____
_____
_____
_____
_____
_____

My two massive goals to focus on today:

1. _____
2. _____

Take three deep "oxytocin breaths" by placing your hand on your heart and exhaling the sound "haaaaa".

My Mind Candy Minute Journal

Date ____/____/_____

"To conquer fear is the beginning of wisdom." - Bertrand Russell

I am grateful for...

1. _____
2. _____
3. _____

Daily affirmations. Mind Candy Voice Note *(Record your affirmations on your smart phone and listen to them several times throughout your day)*

I am... _____

_____
_____
_____
_____
_____
_____

My two massive goals to focus on today:

1. _____
2. _____

Take three deep "oxytocin breaths" by placing your hand on your heart and exhaling the sound "haaaaa".

My Mind Candy Minute Journal

Date ____/____/_____

"Success is every minute you live. It's the process of living. It's stopping for the moments of beauty, of pleasure; the moments of peace. Success is not a destination that you ever reach. Success is the quality of the journey." - Jennifer James

I am grateful for...

1. _____
2. _____
3. _____

Daily affirmations. Mind Candy Voice Note *(Record your affirmations on your smart phone and listen to them several times throughout your day)*

I am... _____

_____
_____
_____
_____
_____
_____
_____

My two massive goals to focus on today:

1. _____
2. _____

Take three deep "oxytocin breaths" by placing your hand on your heart and exhaling the sound "haaaaa".

My Mind Candy Minute Journal

Date ____/____/_____

"Write down the thoughts of the moment. Those that come unsought for are commonly the most valuable." - Francis Bacon

I am grateful for...

1. _____
2. _____
3. _____

Daily affirmations. Mind Candy Voice Note *(Record your affirmations on your smart phone and listen to them several times throughout your day)*

I am... _____

_____
_____
_____
_____
_____
_____

My two massive goals to focus on today:

1. _____
2. _____

Take three deep "oxytocin breaths" by placing your hand on your heart and exhaling the sound "haaaaa".

My Mind Candy Minute Journal

Date ____/____/_____

"It is literally true that you can succeed best and quickest by helping others to succeed." - Napoleon Hill

I am grateful for...

1. _____
2. _____
3. _____

Daily affirmations. Mind Candy Voice Note *(Record your affirmations on your smart phone and listen to them several times throughout your day)*

I am... _____

_____
_____
_____
_____
_____
_____

My two massive goals to focus on today:

1. _____
2. _____

Take three deep "oxytocin breaths" by placing your hand on your heart and exhaling the sound "haaaaa".

My Mind Candy Minute Journal

Date ____/____/_____

"You've got to win in your mind before you win in your life." - John Addison

I am grateful for...

1. _____
2. _____
3. _____

Daily affirmations. Mind Candy Voice Note *(Record your affirmations on your smart phone and listen to them several times throughout your day)*

I am... _____

_____
_____
_____
_____
_____
_____

My two massive goals to focus on today:

1. _____
2. _____

Take three deep "oxytocin breaths" by placing your hand on your heart and exhaling the sound "haaaaa".

My Mind Candy Minute Journal

Date ____/____/_____

"Never be afraid to tread the path alone. Know which is your path and follow is wherever it may lead you; do not feel you have to follow in someone else's footsteps." - Eileen Caddy

I am grateful for...

1. _____
2. _____
3. _____

Daily affirmations. Mind Candy Voice Note *(Record your affirmations on your smart phone and listen to them several times throughout your day)*

I am... _____

_____
_____
_____
_____
_____
_____

My two massive goals to focus on today:

1. _____
2. _____

Take three deep "oxytocin breaths" by placing your hand on your heart and exhaling the sound "haaaaa".

My Mind Candy Minute Journal

Date ____/____/_____

"Success is how high you bounce after you hit bottom." - George Patton

I am grateful for...

1. _____
2. _____
3. _____

Daily affirmations. Mind Candy Voice Note *(Record your affirmations on your smart phone and listen to them several times throughout your day)*

I am... _____
_____
_____
_____
_____
_____
_____

My two massive goals to focus on today:

1. _____
2. _____

Take three deep "oxytocin breaths" by placing your hand on your heart and exhaling the sound "haaaaa".

My Mind Candy Minute Journal

Date ____/____/_____

"The reward of a thing well done is to have done it." - Ralph Waldo Emerson

I am grateful for...

1. _____
2. _____
3. _____

Daily affirmations. Mind Candy Voice Note *(Record your affirmations on your smart phone and listen to them several times throughout your day)*

I am... _____
_____
_____
_____
_____
_____
_____

My two massive goals to focus on today:

1. _____
2. _____

Take three deep "oxytocin breaths" by placing your hand on your heart and exhaling the sound "haaaaa".

My Mind Candy Minute Journal

Date ____/____/_____

"Knowledge without follow-through is worse than no knowledge." - Henry Charles Bukowski

I am grateful for...

1. _____
2. _____
3. _____

Daily affirmations. Mind Candy Voice Note *(Record your affirmations on your smart phone and listen to them several times throughout your day)*

I am... _____

_____
_____
_____
_____
_____
_____

My two massive goals to focus on today:

1. _____
2. _____

Take three deep "oxytocin breaths" by placing your hand on your heart and exhaling the sound "haaaaa".

My Mind Candy Minute Journal

Date ____/____/_____

"Do not despise the bottom rungs in the ascent to greatness." - Publilius Syrus

I am grateful for...

1. _____
2. _____
3. _____

Daily affirmations. Mind Candy Voice Note *(Record your affirmations on your smart phone and listen to them several times throughout your day)*

I am... _____

_____
_____
_____
_____
_____

My two massive goals to focus on today:

1. _____
2. _____

Take three deep "oxytocin breaths" by placing your hand on your heart and exhaling the sound "haaaaa".

My Mind Candy Minute Journal

Date _____/_____/_____

"The merit in action lies in finishing it to the end." - Genghis Khan

I am grateful for...

1. _____
2. _____
3. _____

Daily affirmations. Mind Candy Voice Note *(Record your affirmations on your smart phone and listen to them several times throughout your day)*

I am... _____
_____
_____
_____
_____
_____
_____

My two massive goals to focus on today:

1. _____
2. _____

Take three deep "oxytocin breaths" by placing your hand on your heart and exhaling the sound "haaaaa".

My Mind Candy Minute Journal

Date ____/____/_____

"To move the world we must first move ourselves." - Socrates

I am grateful for...

1. _____
2. _____
3. _____

Daily affirmations. Mind Candy Voice Note *(Record your affirmations on your smart phone and listen to them several times throughout your day)*

I am... _____

_____

_____

_____

_____

_____

_____

My two massive goals to focus on today:

1. _____
2. _____

Take three deep "oxytocin breaths" by placing your hand on your heart and exhaling the sound "haaaaa".

My Mind Candy Minute Journal

Date ____/____/_____

"Make a success of living by seeing the goal and aiming for it unswervingly." - Cecil B. De Mille

I am grateful for...

1. _____
2. _____
3. _____

Daily affirmations. Mind Candy Voice Note *(Record your affirmations on your smart phone and listen to them several times throughout your day)*

I am... _____

_____
_____
_____
_____
_____
_____

My two massive goals to focus on today:

1. _____
2. _____

Take three deep "oxytocin breaths" by placing your hand on your heart and exhaling the sound "haaaaa".

My Mind Candy Minute Journal

Date ____/____/_____

"The man who will use his skill and constructive imagination to see how much he can give for a dollar, instead of how little he can give for a dollar, is bound to succeed." - Henry Ford

I am grateful for...

1. _____
2. _____
3. _____

Daily affirmations. Mind Candy Voice Note *(Record your affirmations on your smart phone and listen to them several times throughout your day)*

I am... _____

_____
_____
_____
_____
_____
_____

My two massive goals to focus on today:

1. _____
2. _____

Take three deep "oxytocin breaths" by placing your hand on your heart and exhaling the sound "haaaaa".

My Mind Candy Minute Journal

Date ____/____/_____

"Optimists are right. So are pessimists. It's up to you to choose which you will be." - Harvey Mackay

I am grateful for...

1. _____
2. _____
3. _____

Daily affirmations. Mind Candy Voice Note *(Record your affirmations on your smart phone and listen to them several times throughout your day)*

I am... _____
_____
_____
_____
_____
_____
_____

My two massive goals to focus on today:

1. _____
2. _____

Take three deep "oxytocin breaths" by placing your hand on your heart and exhaling the sound "haaaaa".

My Mind Candy Minute Journal

Date ____/____/_____

"Many hands and hearts and minds generally contribute to anyone's notable achievements." - Walt Disney

I am grateful for...

1. _____
2. _____
3. _____

Daily affirmations. Mind Candy Voice Note *(Record your affirmations on your smart phone and listen to them several times throughout your day)*

I am... _____

_____
_____
_____
_____
_____
_____

My two massive goals to focus on today:

1. _____
2. _____

Take three deep "oxytocin breaths" by placing your hand on your heart and exhaling the sound "haaaaa".

My Mind Candy Minute Journal

Date ____/____/_____

"Winners are the ones who really listen to the truth of their hearts." - Sylvester Stallone

I am grateful for...

1. _____
2. _____
3. _____

Daily affirmations. Mind Candy Voice Note *(Record your affirmations on your smart phone and listen to them several times throughout your day)*

I am... _____

_____

_____

_____

_____

_____

_____

My two massive goals to focus on today:

1. _____
2. _____

Take three deep "oxytocin breaths" by placing your hand on your heart and exhaling the sound "haaaaa".

My Mind Candy Minute Journal

Date ____/____/_____

"When you miss a shot, never think of what you did wrong. Take the next shot thinking of what you must do right." - Tony Alfonso

I am grateful for...

1. _____
2. _____
3. _____

Daily affirmations. Mind Candy Voice Note *(Record your affirmations on your smart phone and listen to them several times throughout your day)*

I am... _____

_____
_____
_____
_____
_____
_____

My two massive goals to focus on today:

1. _____
2. _____

Take three deep "oxytocin breaths" by placing your hand on your heart and exhaling the sound "haaaaa".

My Mind Candy Minute Journal

Date ____/____/_____

"Winners make a habit of manufacturing their own positive expectations in advance of the event." - Brian Tracy

I am grateful for...

1. _____
2. _____
3. _____

Daily affirmations. Mind Candy Voice Note *(Record your affirmations on your smart phone and listen to them several times throughout your day)*

I am... _____

_____
_____
_____
_____
_____
_____

My two massive goals to focus on today:

1. _____
2. _____

Take three deep "oxytocin breaths" by placing your hand on your heart and exhaling the sound "haaaaa".

My Mind Candy Minute Journal

Date ____/____/_____

"A good criterion for measuring success in life is the number of people you have made happy." - Robert J. Lumsden

I am grateful for...

1. _____
2. _____
3. _____

Daily affirmations. Mind Candy Voice Note *(Record your affirmations on your smart phone and listen to them several times throughout your day)*

I am... _____
_____
_____
_____
_____
_____
_____

My two massive goals to focus on today:

1. _____
2. _____

Take three deep "oxytocin breaths" by placing your hand on your heart and exhaling the sound "haaaaa".

My Mind Candy Minute Journal

Date ____/____/_____

"The history of the world is the history of a few people who had faith in themselves." - Swami Vivekananda

I am grateful for...

1. _____
2. _____
3. _____

Daily affirmations. Mind Candy Voice Note *(Record your affirmations on your smart phone and listen to them several times throughout your day.)*

I am... _____

_____

_____

_____

_____

_____

_____

My two massive goals to focus on today:

1. _____
2. _____

Take three deep "oxytocin breaths" by placing your hand on your heart and exhaling the sound "haaaaa".

My Mind Candy Minute Journal

Date ____/____/_____

"Ability may take you to the top, but it takes character to stay there." - William Blake

I am grateful for...

1. _____
2. _____
3. _____

Daily affirmations. Mind Candy Voice Note *(Record your affirmations on your smart phone and listen to them several times throughout your day)*

I am... _____

_____

_____

_____

_____

_____

_____

My two massive goals to focus on today:

1. _____
2. _____

Take three deep "oxytocin breaths" by placing your hand on your heart and exhaling the sound "haaaaa".

My Mind Candy Minute Journal

Date ____/____/_____

"Success is the progressive realization of worthwhile, predetermined, personal goals." - Paul J. Meyer

I am grateful for...

1. _____
2. _____
3. _____

Daily affirmations. Mind Candy Voice Note *(Record your affirmations on your smart phone and listen to them several times throughout your day)*

I am... _____

_____

_____

_____

_____

_____

_____

My two massive goals to focus on today:

1. _____
2. _____

Take three deep "oxytocin breaths" by placing your hand on your heart and exhaling the sound "haaaaa".

My Mind Candy Minute Journal

Date ____/____/_____

"Why not go out on a limb? Isn't that where the fruit is?" - Frank Scully

I am grateful for...

1. _____
2. _____
3. _____

Daily affirmations. Mind Candy Voice Note *(Record your affirmations on your smart phone and listen to them several times throughout your day)*

I am... _____

_____
_____
_____
_____
_____
_____

My two massive goals to focus on today:

1. _____
2. _____

Take three deep "oxytocin breaths" by placing your hand on your heart and exhaling the sound "haaaaa".

My Mind Candy Minute Journal

Date ____/____/_____

"Success is to be measured not so much by the position that one has reached in life as by the obstacles which he has overcome while trying to succeed." - Booker T. Washington

I am grateful for...

1. _____
2. _____
3. _____

Daily affirmations. Mind Candy Voice Note *(Record your affirmations on your smart phone and listen to them several times throughout your day)*

I am... _____

_____

_____

_____

_____

_____

My two massive goals to focus on today:

1. _____
2. _____

Take three deep "oxytocin breaths" by placing your hand on your heart and exhaling the sound "haaaaa".

My Mind Candy Minute Journal

Date ____/____/_____

"The secret of success is consistency of purpose." - Benjamin Disraeli

I am grateful for...

1. _____
2. _____
3. _____

Daily affirmations. Mind Candy Voice Note *(Record your affirmations on your smart phone and listen to them several times throughout your day)*

I am... _____

_____
_____
_____
_____
_____
_____

My two massive goals to focus on today:

1. _____
2. _____

Take three deep "oxytocin breaths" by placing your hand on your heart and exhaling the sound "haaaaa".

My Mind Candy Minute Journal

Date ____/____/_____

"It's not that I'm so smart; it's just that I stay with problems longer." - Albert Einstein

I am grateful for...

1. _____
2. _____
3. _____

Daily affirmations. Mind Candy Voice Note *(Record your affirmations on your smart phone and listen to them several times throughout your day)*

I am... _____

_____
_____
_____
_____
_____
_____

My two massive goals to focus on today:

1. _____
2. _____

Take three deep "oxytocin breaths" by placing your hand on your heart and exhaling the sound "haaaaa".

My Mind Candy Minute Journal

Date ____/____/_____

"We are what we repeatedly do. Excellence then is not an act but a habit." - Aristotle

I am grateful for...

1. _____
2. _____
3. _____

Daily affirmations. Mind Candy Voice Note *(Record your affirmations on your smart phone and listen to them several times throughout your day)*

I am... _____
_____
_____
_____
_____
_____
_____

My two massive goals to focus on today:

1. _____
2. _____

Take three deep "oxytocin breaths" by placing your hand on your heart and exhaling the sound "haaaaa".

My Mind Candy Minute Journal

Date _____/_____/_____

"Sometimes our best is simply not enough. We have to do what is required." - Sir Winston Churchill

I am grateful for...

1. _____
2. _____
3. _____

Daily affirmations. Mind Candy Voice Note *(Record your affirmations on your smart phone and listen to them several times throughout your day)*

I am... _____
_____
_____
_____
_____
_____
_____

My two massive goals to focus on today:

1. _____
2. _____

Take three deep "oxytocin breaths" by placing your hand on your heart and exhaling the sound "haaaaa".

My Mind Candy Minute Journal

Date ____/____/_____

"The path to success is to take massive, determined action." - Anthony Robbins

I am grateful for...

1. _____
2. _____
3. _____

Daily affirmations. Mind Candy Voice Note *(Record your affirmations on your smart phone and listen to them several times throughout your day)*

I am... _____

_____

_____

_____

_____

_____

My two massive goals to focus on today:

1. _____
2. _____

Take three deep "oxytocin breaths" by placing your hand on your heart and exhaling the sound "haaaaa".

My Mind Candy Minute Journal

Date ____/____/_____

"Live out of your imagination, not your history." - Stephen Covey

I am grateful for...

1. _____
2. _____
3. _____

Daily affirmations. Mind Candy Voice Note *(Record your affirmations on your smart phone and listen to them several times throughout your day)*

I am... _____

_____

_____

_____

_____

_____

_____

My two massive goals to focus on today:

1. _____
2. _____

Take three deep "oxytocin breaths" by placing your hand
on your heart and exhaling the sound "haaaaa".

My Mind Candy Minute Journal

Date ____/____/_____

"Perpetual optimism is a force multiplier." - Colin Powell

I am grateful for...

1. _____
2. _____
3. _____

Daily affirmations. Mind Candy Voice Note *(Record your affirmations on your smart phone and listen to them several times throughout your day)*

I am... _____

_____

_____

_____

_____

_____

_____

My two massive goals to focus on today:

1. _____
2. _____

Take three deep "oxytocin breaths" by placing your hand on your heart and exhaling the sound "haaaaa".

My Mind Candy Minute Journal

Date ____/____/_____

"Forget yourself and start to work." - Gordon B. Hinckley

I am grateful for...

1. _____
2. _____
3. _____

Daily affirmations. Mind Candy Voice Note *(Record your affirmations on your smart phone and listen to them several times throughout your day)*

I am... _____

_____

_____

_____

_____

_____

My two massive goals to focus on today:

1. _____
2. _____

Take three deep "oxytocin breaths" by placing your hand on your heart and exhaling the sound "haaaaa".

My Mind Candy Minute Journal

Date ____/____/_____

"Our business in life is not to get ahead of others, but to get ahead of ourselves." - Zig Ziglar

I am grateful for...

1. _____
2. _____
3. _____

Daily affirmations. Mind Candy Voice Note *(Record your affirmations on your smart phone and listen to them several times throughout your day)*

I am... _____

_____
_____
_____
_____
_____
_____

My two massive goals to focus on today:

1. _____
2. _____

Take three deep "oxytocin breaths" by placing your hand on your heart and exhaling the sound "haaaaa".

My Mind Candy Minute Journal

Date ____/____/_____

"Always bear in mind that our own resolution to succeed is more important than any other one thing." - Abraham Lincoln

I am grateful for...

1. _____
2. _____
3. _____

Daily affirmations. Mind Candy Voice Note *(Record your affirmations on your smart phone and listen to them several times throughout your day)*

I am... _____
_____
_____
_____
_____
_____
_____

My two massive goals to focus on today:

1. _____
2. _____

Take three deep "oxytocin breaths" by placing your hand on your heart and exhaling the sound "haaaaa".

My Mind Candy Minute Journal

Date ____/____/_____

"One must have strategies to execute dreams." - Azim Premji

I am grateful for...

1. _____
2. _____
3. _____

Daily affirmations. Mind Candy Voice Note *(Record your affirmations on your smart phone and listen to them several times throughout your day)*

I am... _____

_____
_____
_____
_____
_____
_____

My two massive goals to focus on today:

1. _____
2. _____

Take three deep "oxytocin breaths" by placing your hand on your heart and exhaling the sound "haaaaa".

My Mind Candy Minute Journal

Date ____/____/_____

"Try to forget yourself in the service of others. For when we think too much of ourselves and our own interests, we easily become despondent. But when we work for others, our efforts return to bless us." - Sidney Powell

I am grateful for...

1. _____
2. _____
3. _____

Daily affirmations. Mind Candy Voice Note *(Record your affirmations on your smart phone and listen to them several times throughout your day)*

I am... _____

_____
_____
_____
_____
_____
_____

My two massive goals to focus on today:

1. _____
2. _____

Take three deep "oxytocin breaths" by placing your hand on your heart and exhaling the sound "haaaaa".

My Mind Candy Minute Journal

Date ____/____/_____

"Opportunities multiply as they are seized." - Sun Tzu

I am grateful for...

1. _____
2. _____
3. _____

Daily affirmations. Mind Candy Voice Note *(Record your affirmations on your smart phone and listen to them several times throughout your day)*

I am... _____

_____

_____

_____

_____

_____

_____

My two massive goals to focus on today:

1. _____
2. _____

Take three deep "oxytocin breaths" by placing your hand on your heart and exhaling the sound "haaaaa".

My Mind Candy Minute Journal

Date ____/____/_____

"Nothing is so contagious as enthusiasm. It moves stones, it charms brutes. Enthusiasm is the genius of sincerity, and truth accomplishes no victories without it." - Edward Bulwer-Lytton

I am grateful for...

1. _____
2. _____
3. _____

Daily affirmations. Mind Candy Voice Note *(Record your affirmations on your smart phone and listen to them several times throughout your day)*

I am... _____

_____
_____
_____
_____
_____
_____

My two massive goals to focus on today:

1. _____
2. _____

Take three deep "oxytocin breaths" by placing your hand on your heart and exhaling the sound "haaaaa".

My Mind Candy Minute Journal

Date _____/_____/_____

"Each problem that I solved became a rule which served afterwards to solve other problems." - Rene Descartes

I am grateful for...

1. _____
2. _____
3. _____

Daily affirmations. Mind Candy Voice Note *(Record your affirmations on your smart phone and listen to them several times throughout your day)*

I am... _____

_____
_____
_____
_____
_____
_____

My two massive goals to focus on today:

1. _____
2. _____

Take three deep "oxytocin breaths" by placing your hand on your heart and exhaling the sound "haaaaa".

My Mind Candy Minute Journal

Date ____/____/_____

"Success equals goals... all else is commentary." - Brian Tracy

I am grateful for...

1. _____
2. _____
3. _____

Daily affirmations. Mind Candy Voice Note *(Record your affirmations on your smart phone and listen to them several times throughout your day)*

I am... _____

_____

_____

_____

_____

_____

_____

My two massive goals to focus on today:

1. _____
2. _____

Take three deep "oxytocin breaths" by placing your hand on your heart and exhaling the sound "haaaaa".

My Mind Candy Minute Journal

Date ____/____/_____

"If you aren't making any mistakes, it's a sure sign you're playing it too safe." - John Maxwell

I am grateful for...

1. _____
2. _____
3. _____

Daily affirmations. Mind Candy Voice Note *(Record your affirmations on your smart phone and listen to them several times throughout your day)*

I am... _____

_____

_____

_____

_____

_____

_____

My two massive goals to focus on today:

1. _____
2. _____

Take three deep "oxytocin breaths" by placing your hand on your heart and exhaling the sound "haaaaa".

My Mind Candy Minute Journal

Date ____/____/_____

"I don't know the key to success, but the key to failure is trying to please everybody." - Bill Cosby

I am grateful for...

1. _____
2. _____
3. _____

Daily affirmations. Mind Candy Voice Note *(Record your affirmations on your smart phone and listen to them several times throughout your day.)*

I am... _____

_____
_____
_____
_____
_____
_____

My two massive goals to focus on today:

1. _____
2. _____

Take three deep "oxytocin breaths" by placing your hand on your heart and exhaling the sound "haaaaa".

My Mind Candy Minute Journal

Date ____/____/_____

"The dictionary is the only place where success comes before work." - Arthur Brisbane

I am grateful for...

1. _____
2. _____
3. _____

Daily affirmations. Mind Candy Voice Note *(Record your affirmations on your smart phone and listen to them several times throughout your day)*

I am... _____

_____
_____
_____
_____
_____
_____

My two massive goals to focus on today:

1. _____
2. _____

Take three deep "oxytocin breaths" by placing your hand on your heart and exhaling the sound "haaaaa".

My Mind Candy Minute Journal

Date _____/_____/_____

"Striving for success without hard work is like trying to harvest where you haven't planted." - David Bly

I am grateful for...

1. _____
2. _____
3. _____

Daily affirmations. Mind Candy Voice Note *(Record your affirmations on your smart phone and listen to them several times throughout your day.)*

I am... _____

_____
_____
_____
_____
_____
_____

My two massive goals to focus on today:

1. _____
2. _____

Take three deep "oxytocin breaths" by placing your hand on your heart and exhaling the sound "haaaaa".

My Mind Candy Minute Journal

Date ____/____/_____

"As long as you are going to be thinking anyway, think big." - Donald Trump

I am grateful for...

1. _____
2. _____
3. _____

Daily affirmations. Mind Candy Voice Note *(Record your affirmations on your smart phone and listen to them several times throughout your day)*

I am... _____

_____

_____

_____

_____

_____

_____

My two massive goals to focus on today:

1. _____
2. _____

Take three deep "oxytocin breaths" by placing your hand on your heart and exhaling the sound "haaaaa".

My Mind Candy Minute Journal

Date ____/____/_____

*"Success is the sum of small efforts repeated
day in and day out." - Robert Collier*

I am grateful for...

1. _____
2. _____
3. _____

Daily affirmations. Mind Candy Voice Note *(Record your affirmations on your smart phone and listen to them several times throughout your day)*

I am... _____
_____
_____
_____
_____
_____
_____

My two massive goals to focus on today:

1. _____
2. _____

Take three deep "oxytocin breaths" by placing your hand
on your heart and exhaling the sound "haaaaa".

My Mind Candy Minute Journal

Date ____/____/_____

"No man is ever whipped until he quits - in his own mind." - Napoleon Hill

I am grateful for...

1. _____
2. _____
3. _____

Daily affirmations. Mind Candy Voice Note *(Record your affirmations on your smart phone and listen to them several times throughout your day)*

I am... _____

_____
_____
_____
_____
_____
_____
_____

My two massive goals to focus on today:

1. _____
2. _____

Take three deep "oxytocin breaths" by placing your hand on your heart and exhaling the sound "haaaaa".

My Mind Candy Minute Journal

Date ____/____/_____

"Success is 20% skills and 80% strategy. You might know how to read, but more importantly, what's your plan to read?" - Jim Rohn

I am grateful for...

1. _____
2. _____
3. _____

Daily affirmations. Mind Candy Voice Note *(Record your affirmations on your smart phone and listen to them several times throughout your day)*

I am... _____

_____
_____
_____
_____
_____
_____
_____

My two massive goals to focus on today:

1. _____
2. _____

Take three deep "oxytocin breaths" by placing your hand on your heart and exhaling the sound "haaaaa".

My Mind Candy Minute Journal

Date ____/____/_____

"Be who you are and say what you feel, because those who mind don't matter and those who matter don't mind." - Dr. Suess

I am grateful for...

1. _____
2. _____
3. _____

Daily affirmations. Mind Candy Voice Note *(Record your affirmations on your smart phone and listen to them several times throughout your day)*

I am... _____

_____
_____
_____
_____
_____
_____

My two massive goals to focus on today:

1. _____
2. _____

Take three deep "oxytocin breaths" by placing your hand on your heart and exhaling the sound "haaaaa".

My Mind Candy Minute Journal

Date ____/____/_____

"People rarely succeed unless they have fun in what they are doing." - Dale Carnegie

I am grateful for...

1. _____
2. _____
3. _____

Daily affirmations. Mind Candy Voice Note *(Record your affirmations on your smart phone and listen to them several times throughout your day)*

I am... _____

_____
_____
_____
_____
_____
_____

My two massive goals to focus on today:

1. _____
2. _____

Take three deep "oxytocin breaths" by placing your hand on your heart and exhaling the sound "haaaaa".

My Mind Candy Minute Journal

Date ____/____/_____

"Enter every activity without giving mental recognition to the possibility of defeat. Concentrate on your strengths, instead of your weaknesses ... on your powers, instead of your problems." - Paul J. Meyer

I am grateful for...

1. _____
2. _____
3. _____

Daily affirmations. Mind Candy Voice Note *(Record your affirmations on your smart phone and listen to them several times throughout your day)*

I am... _____

_____

_____

_____

_____

_____

_____

My two massive goals to focus on today:

1. _____
2. _____

Take three deep "oxytocin breaths" by placing your hand on your heart and exhaling the sound "haaaaa".

My Mind Candy Minute Journal

Date _____/_____/_____

"People with goals succeed because they know where they're going." - Earl Nightingale

I am grateful for...

1. _____
2. _____
3. _____

Daily affirmations. Mind Candy Voice Note *(Record your affirmations on your smart phone and listen to them several times throughout your day)*

I am... _____

_____
_____
_____
_____
_____
_____

My two massive goals to focus on today:

1. _____
2. _____

Take three deep "oxytocin breaths" by placing your hand on your heart and exhaling the sound "haaaaa".

My Mind Candy Minute Journal

Date ____/____/_____

"Thoughts and ideas are the source of all wealth, success, material gain, all great discoveries, inventions and achievement." - Mark Victor Hansen

I am grateful for...

1. _____
2. _____
3. _____

Daily affirmations. Mind Candy Voice Note *(Record your affirmations on your smart phone and listen to them several times throughout your day)*

I am... _____
_____
_____
_____
_____
_____
_____

My two massive goals to focus on today:

1. _____
2. _____

Take three deep "oxytocin breaths" by placing your hand on your heart and exhaling the sound "haaaaa".

My Mind Candy Minute Journal

Date ____/____/_____

"The secret of business is to know something that nobody else knows." - Aristotle Onansis

I am grateful for...

1. _____
2. _____
3. _____

Daily affirmations. Mind Candy Voice Note *(Record your affirmations on your smart phone and listen to them several times throughout your day)*

I am... _____

_____
_____
_____
_____
_____
_____

My two massive goals to focus on today:

1. _____
2. _____

Take three deep "oxytocin breaths" by placing your hand on your heart and exhaling the sound "haaaaa".

My Mind Candy Minute Journal

Date ____/____/_____

"In life, as in a football game, the principle to follow is: Hit the line hard." - Theodore Roosevelt

I am grateful for...

1. _____
2. _____
3. _____

Daily affirmations. Mind Candy Voice Note *(Record your affirmations on your smart phone and listen to them several times throughout your day)*

I am... _____

_____
_____
_____
_____
_____
_____

My two massive goals to focus on today:

1. _____
2. _____

Take three deep "oxytocin breaths" by placing your hand on your heart and exhaling the sound "haaaaa".

My Mind Candy Minute Journal

Date ____/____/_____

"If you go to work on your goals, your goals will go to work on you. If you go to work on your plan, your plan will go to work on you. Whatever good things we build end up building us." - Jim Rohn

I am grateful for...

1. _____
2. _____
3. _____

Daily affirmations. Mind Candy Voice Note *(Record your affirmations on your smart phone and listen to them several times throughout your day)*

I am... _____

_____
_____
_____
_____
_____
_____

My two massive goals to focus on today:

1. _____
2. _____

Take three deep "oxytocin breaths" by placing your hand on your heart and exhaling the sound "haaaaa".

My Mind Candy Minute Journal

Date ____/____/_____

"If one advances confidently in the direction of his dreams, and endeavors to live the life which he has imagined, he will meet with a success unexpected in common hours." - Henry David Thoreau

I am grateful for...

1. _____
2. _____
3. _____

Daily affirmations. Mind Candy Voice Note *(Record your affirmations on your smart phone and listen to them several times throughout your day)*

I am... _____

_____

_____

_____

_____

_____

_____

My two massive goals to focus on today:

1. _____
2. _____

Take three deep "oxytocin breaths" by placing your hand on your heart and exhaling the sound "haaaaa".

My Mind Candy Minute Journal

Date _____/_____/_____

"Successful leaders see the opportunities in every difficulty rather than the difficulty in every opportunity." - Reed Markham

I am grateful for...

1. _____
2. _____
3. _____

Daily affirmations. Mind Candy Voice Note *(Record your affirmations on your smart phone and listen to them several times throughout your day)*

I am... _____

_____
_____
_____
_____
_____
_____

My two massive goals to focus on today:

1. _____
2. _____

Take three deep "oxytocin breaths" by placing your hand on your heart and exhaling the sound "haaaaa".

My Mind Candy Minute Journal

Date ____/____/_____

"When you're going through hell, keep going." - Albert Einstein

I am grateful for...

1. _____
2. _____
3. _____

Daily affirmations. Mind Candy Voice Note *(Record your affirmations on your smart phone and listen to them several times throughout your day)*

I am... _____

_____

_____

_____

_____

_____

_____

My two massive goals to focus on today:

1. _____
2. _____

Take three deep "oxytocin breaths" by placing your hand on your heart and exhaling the sound "haaaaa".

My Mind Candy Minute Journal

Date ____/____/_____

"Any idea that is held in the mind that is either feared or revered will, begin at once to clothe itself in the most convenient and appropriate physical forms available." - Andrew Carnegie

I am grateful for...

1. _____
2. _____
3. _____

Daily affirmations. Mind Candy Voice Note *(Record your affirmations on your smart phone and listen to them several times throughout your day)*

I am... _____

_____
_____
_____
_____
_____
_____

My two massive goals to focus on today:

1. _____
2. _____

Take three deep "oxytocin breaths" by placing your hand on your heart and exhaling the sound "haaaaa".

My Mind Candy Minute Journal

Date ____/____/_____

"If you can imagine it, you can create it. If you can dream it, you can become it." - William Arthur Ward

I am grateful for...

1. _____
2. _____
3. _____

Daily affirmations. Mind Candy Voice Note *(Record your affirmations on your smart phone and listen to them several times throughout your day)*

I am... _____

_____
_____
_____
_____
_____
_____

My two massive goals to focus on today:

1. _____
2. _____

Take three deep "oxytocin breaths" by placing your hand on your heart and exhaling the sound "haaaaa".

My Mind Candy Minute Journal

Date ____/____/_____

"Our doubts are traitors and make us lose the good that we oft may win by fearing to attempt." - William Shakespeare

I am grateful for...

1. _____
2. _____
3. _____

Daily affirmations. Mind Candy Voice Note *(Record your affirmations on your smart phone and listen to them several times throughout your day)*

I am... _____

_____

_____

_____

_____

_____

_____

My two massive goals to focus on today:

1. _____
2. _____

Take three deep "oxytocin breaths" by placing your hand on your heart and exhaling the sound "haaaaa".

My Mind Candy Minute Journal

Date ____/____/_____

"There is only one way to succeed in anything, and that is to give it everything." - Vince Lombardi

I am grateful for...

1. _____
2. _____
3. _____

Daily affirmations. Mind Candy Voice Note *(Record your affirmations on your smart phone and listen to them several times throughout your day)*

I am... _____

_____
_____
_____
_____
_____
_____

My two massive goals to focus on today:

1. _____
2. _____

Take three deep "oxytocin breaths" by placing your hand on your heart and exhaling the sound "haaaaa".

My Mind Candy Minute Journal

Date ____/____/_____

"Success is not the key to happiness. Happiness is the key to success. If you love what you are doing, you will be successful." - Albert Schweitzer

I am grateful for...

1. _____
2. _____
3. _____

Daily affirmations. Mind Candy Voice Note *(Record your affirmations on your smart phone and listen to them several times throughout your day)*

I am... _____

_____
_____
_____
_____
_____
_____

My two massive goals to focus on today:

1. _____
2. _____

Take three deep "oxytocin breaths" by placing your hand on your heart and exhaling the sound "haaaaa".

My Mind Candy Minute Journal

Date ____/____/_____

"Success... it's what you do with what you've got." - Leroy Van Dyke

I am grateful for...

1. _____
2. _____
3. _____

Daily affirmations. Mind Candy Voice Note *(Record your affirmations on your smart phone and listen to them several times throughout your day)*

I am... _____

_____
_____
_____
_____
_____
_____

My two massive goals to focus on today:

1. _____
2. _____

Take three deep "oxytocin breaths" by placing your hand on your heart and exhaling the sound "haaaaa".

My Mind Candy Minute Journal

Date _____/_____/_____

"Behind every successful man there's a lot of unsuccessful years." - Bob Brown

I am grateful for...

1. _____
2. _____
3. _____

Daily affirmations. Mind Candy Voice Note *(Record your affirmations on your smart phone and listen to them several times throughout your day)*

I am... _____

_____

_____

_____

_____

_____

_____

My two massive goals to focus on today:

1. _____
2. _____

Take three deep "oxytocin breaths" by placing your hand on your heart and exhaling the sound "haaaaa".

My Mind Candy Minute Journal

Date ____/____/_____

"The pessimist sees difficulty in every opportunity. The optimist sees opportunity in every difficulty." - Winston Churchill

I am grateful for...

1. _____
2. _____
3. _____

Daily affirmations. Mind Candy Voice Note *(Record your affirmations on your smart phone and listen to them several times throughout your day)*

I am... _____

_____
_____
_____
_____
_____
_____

My two massive goals to focus on today:

1. _____
2. _____

Take three deep "oxytocin breaths" by placing your hand on your heart and exhaling the sound "haaaaa".

My Mind Candy Minute Journal

Date _____/_____/_____

"Every evening, write down the six most important things that you must do the next day. Then while you sleep your subconscious will work on the best ways for you to accomplish them. Your next day will go much more smoothly." - Tom Hopkins

I am grateful for...

1. _____
2. _____
3. _____

Daily affirmations. Mind Candy Voice Note *(Record your affirmations on your smart phone and listen to them several times throughout your day)*

I am... _____

_____
_____
_____
_____
_____
_____

My two massive goals to focus on today:

1. _____
2. _____

Take three deep "oxytocin breaths" by placing your hand on your heart and exhaling the sound "haaaaa".

My Mind Candy Minute Journal

Date ____/____/_____

"Never turn down a job because you think it's too small, you don't know where it can lead." - Julia Morgan

I am grateful for...

1. _____
2. _____
3. _____

Daily affirmations. Mind Candy Voice Note *(Record your affirmations on your smart phone and listen to them several times throughout your day)*

I am... _____

_____
_____
_____
_____
_____
_____

My two massive goals to focus on today:

1. _____
2. _____

Take three deep "oxytocin breaths" by placing your hand on your heart and exhaling the sound "haaaaa".

My Mind Candy Minute Journal

Date _____/_____/_____

"The test of a successful person is not an ability to eliminate all problems before they arise, but to meet and work out difficulties when they do arise. We must be willing to make an intelligent compromise with perfection lest we wait forever before taking action. It's still good advice to cross bridges as we come to them." - David Schwartz

I am grateful for...

1. _____
2. _____
3. _____

Daily affirmations. Mind Candy Voice Note *(Record your affirmations on your smart phone and listen to them several times throughout your day)*

I am... _____

_____

_____

_____

_____

_____

_____

My two massive goals to focus on today:

1. _____
2. _____

Take three deep "oxytocin breaths" by placing your hand on your heart and exhaling the sound "haaaaa".

My Mind Candy Minute Journal

Date ____/____/_____

"For it matters not how small the beginning may seem to be. What is once well done, is well done forever." - Henry David Thoreau

I am grateful for...

1. _____
2. _____
3. _____

Daily affirmations. Mind Candy Voice Note *(Record your affirmations on your smart phone and listen to them several times throughout your day)*

I am... _____

_____
_____
_____
_____
_____
_____

My two massive goals to focus on today:

1. _____
2. _____

Take three deep "oxytocin breaths" by placing your hand on your heart and exhaling the sound "haaaaa".

My Mind Candy Minute Journal

Date _____/_____/_____

"People are always blaming circumstances for what they are. I don't believe in circumstances. The people who get on in this world are the people who get up and look for the circumstances they want and if they can't find them, make them." - George Bernard Shaw

I am grateful for...

1. _____
2. _____
3. _____

Daily affirmations. Mind Candy Voice Note *(Record your affirmations on your smart phone and listen to them several times throughout your day)*

I am... _____

_____
_____
_____
_____
_____
_____

My two massive goals to focus on today:

1. _____
2. _____

Take three deep "oxytocin breaths" by placing your hand on your heart and exhaling the sound "haaaaa".

My Mind Candy Minute Journal

Date ____/____/_____

"Develop success from failures. Discouragement and failure are two of the surest stepping stones to success." - Dale Carnegie

I am grateful for...

1. _____
2. _____
3. _____

Daily affirmations. Mind Candy Voice Note *(Record your affirmations on your smart phone and listen to them several times throughout your day)*

I am... _____

_____

_____

_____

_____

_____

_____

My two massive goals to focus on today:

1. _____
2. _____

Take three deep "oxytocin breaths" by placing your hand on your heart and exhaling the sound "haaaaa".

My Mind Candy Minute Journal

Date ____/____/_____

"If you think you can, you can. And if you think you can't, you're right." - Henry Ford

I am grateful for...

1. _____
2. _____
3. _____

Daily affirmations. Mind Candy Voice Note *(Record your affirmations on your smart phone and listen to them several times throughout your day)*

I am... _____

_____

_____

_____

_____

_____

_____

My two massive goals to focus on today:

1. _____
2. _____

Take three deep "oxytocin breaths" by placing your hand on your heart and exhaling the sound "haaaaa".

My Mind Candy Minute Journal

Date ____/____/_____

"He who has never failed somewhere, that man cannot be great." - Herman Melville

I am grateful for...

1. _____
2. _____
3. _____

Daily affirmations. Mind Candy Voice Note *(Record your affirmations on your smart phone and listen to them several times throughout your day)*

I am... _____

_____

_____

_____

_____

_____

_____

My two massive goals to focus on today:

1. _____
2. _____

Take three deep "oxytocin breaths" by placing your hand on your heart and exhaling the sound "haaaaa".

My Mind Candy Minute Journal

Date ____/____/_____

"Recipe for success: Study while others are sleeping; work while others are loafing; prepare while others are playing; and dream while others are wishing." - William A. Ward

I am grateful for...

1. _____
2. _____
3. _____

Daily affirmations. Mind Candy Voice Note *(Record your affirmations on your smart phone and listen to them several times throughout your day)*

I am... _____

_____
_____
_____
_____
_____
_____
_____

My two massive goals to focus on today:

1. _____
2. _____

Take three deep "oxytocin breaths" by placing your hand on your heart and exhaling the sound "haaaaa".

My Mind Candy Minute Journal

Date ____/____/_____

"Success is not so much what we have, as it is what we are." - Jim Rohn

I am grateful for...

1. _____
2. _____
3. _____

Daily affirmations. Mind Candy Voice Note *(Record your affirmations on your smart phone and listen to them several times throughout your day)*

I am... _____

_____

_____

_____

_____

_____

_____

My two massive goals to focus on today:

1. _____
2. _____

Take three deep "oxytocin breaths" by placing your hand on your heart and exhaling the sound "haaaaa".

My Mind Candy Minute Journal

Date ____/____/_____

"Hold a picture of yourself long and steadily enough in your mind's eye, and you will be drawn toward it. If you do not conquer self, you will be conquered by self. The ladder of success is never crowded at the top." - Napoleon Hill

I am grateful for...

1. _____
2. _____
3. _____

Daily affirmations. Mind Candy Voice Note *(Record your affirmations on your smart phone and listen to them several times throughout your day)*

I am... _____

_____
_____
_____
_____
_____
_____

My two massive goals to focus on today:

1. _____
2. _____

Take three deep "oxytocin breaths" by placing your hand on your heart and exhaling the sound "haaaaa".

My Mind Candy Minute Journal

Date ____/____/_____

"The future belongs to those who believe in the beauty of their dreams." - Eleanor Roosevelt

I am grateful for...

1. _____
2. _____
3. _____

Daily affirmations. Mind Candy Voice Note *(Record your affirmations on your smart phone and listen to them several times throughout your day)*

I am... _____

_____

_____

_____

_____

_____

My two massive goals to focus on today:

1. _____
2. _____

Take three deep "oxytocin breaths" by placing your hand on your heart and exhaling the sound "haaaaa".

My Mind Candy Minute Journal

Date ____/____/_____

"Well done is better than well said." - Benjamin Franklin

I am grateful for...

1. _____
2. _____
3. _____

Daily affirmations. Mind Candy Voice Note *(Record your affirmations on your smart phone and listen to them several times throughout your day)*

I am... _____

_____
_____
_____
_____
_____
_____

My two massive goals to focus on today:

1. _____
2. _____

Take three deep "oxytocin breaths" by placing your hand
on your heart and exhaling the sound "haaaaa".

My Mind Candy Minute Journal

Date ____/____/_____

"Success is going from failure to failure without loss of enthusiasm." - Winston Churchill

I am grateful for...

1. _____
2. _____
3. _____

Daily affirmations. Mind Candy Voice Note *(Record your affirmations on your smart phone and listen to them several times throughout your day)*

I am... _____

_____
_____
_____
_____
_____

My two massive goals to focus on today:

1. _____
2. _____

Take three deep "oxytocin breaths" by placing your hand on your heart and exhaling the sound "haaaaa".

My Mind Candy Minute Journal

Date ____/____/_____

"The real secret to success is enthusiasm." - Walter Chrysler

I am grateful for...

1. _____
2. _____
3. _____

Daily affirmations. Mind Candy Voice Note *(Record your affirmations on your smart phone and listen to them several times throughout your day)*

I am... _____

_____

_____

_____

_____

_____

_____

My two massive goals to focus on today:

1. _____
2. _____

Take three deep "oxytocin breaths" by placing your hand on your heart and exhaling the sound "haaaaa".

My Mind Candy Minute Journal

Date ____/____/_____

"Those who have attained things worth having in this world have worked while others idled, have persevered while others gave up in despair, have practiced the valuable habits of self-denial, industry, and singleness of purpose." - Grenville Kleiser

I am grateful for...

1. _____
2. _____
3. _____

Daily affirmations. Mind Candy Voice Note *(Record your affirmations on your smart phone and listen to them several times throughout your day)*

I am... _____

_____
_____
_____
_____
_____
_____

My two massive goals to focus on today:

1. _____
2. _____

Take three deep "oxytocin breaths" by placing your hand on your heart and exhaling the sound "haaaaa".

My Mind Candy Minute Journal

Date _____/_____/_____

"Be bold and mighty forces will come to your aid." - Basil King

I am grateful for...

1. _____
2. _____
3. _____

Daily affirmations. Mind Candy Voice Note *(Record your affirmations on your smart phone and listen to them several times throughout your day)*

I am... _____

_____

_____

_____

_____

_____

My two massive goals to focus on today:

1. _____
2. _____

Take three deep "oxytocin breaths" by placing your hand on your heart and exhaling the sound "haaaaa".

My Mind Candy Minute Journal

Date ____/____/_____

"To be a champion, you have to believe in yourself when nobody else will." - Sugar Ray Robinson

I am grateful for...

1. _____
2. _____
3. _____

Daily affirmations. Mind Candy Voice Note *(Record your affirmations on your smart phone and listen to them several times throughout your day)*

I am... _____

_____

_____

_____

_____

_____

My two massive goals to focus on today:

1. _____
2. _____

Take three deep "oxytocin breaths" by placing your hand on your heart and exhaling the sound "haaaaa".

My Mind Candy Minute Journal

Date ____/____/_____

"Most people give up just when they're about to achieve success. They quit on the one yard line. They give up at the last minute of the game, one foot from a winning touchdown." - Ross Perot

I am grateful for...

1. _____
2. _____
3. _____

Daily affirmations. Mind Candy Voice Note *(Record your affirmations on your smart phone and listen to them several times throughout your day)*

I am... _____

_____
_____
_____
_____
_____
_____

My two massive goals to focus on today:

1. _____
2. _____

Take three deep "oxytocin breaths" by placing your hand on your heart and exhaling the sound "haaaaa".

My Mind Candy Minute Journal

Date ____/____/_____

"People of mediocre ability sometimes achieve outstanding success because they don't know when to quit. Most men succeed because they are determined to." - George E. Allen

I am grateful for...

1. _____
2. _____
3. _____

Daily affirmations. Mind Candy Voice Note *(Record your affirmations on your smart phone and listen to them several times throughout your day)*

I am... _____
_____
_____
_____
_____
_____
_____

My two massive goals to focus on today:

1. _____
2. _____

Take three deep "oxytocin breaths" by placing your hand on your heart and exhaling the sound "haaaaa".

My Mind Candy Minute Journal

Date ____/____/_____

"If you envy successful people, you create a negative force field of attraction that repels you from ever doing the things that you need to do to be successful. If you admire successful people, you create a positive force field of attraction that draws you toward becoming more and more like the kinds of people that you want to be like." - Brian Tracy

I am grateful for...

1. _____
2. _____
3. _____

Daily affirmations. Mind Candy Voice Note *(Record your affirmations on your smart phone and listen to them several times throughout your day)*

I am... _____

_____
_____
_____
_____
_____
_____

My two massive goals to focus on today:

1. _____
2. _____

Take three deep "oxytocin breaths" by placing your hand on your heart and exhaling the sound "haaaaa".

My Mind Candy Minute Journal

Date ____/____/_____

*"It is in your moments of decision that your
destiny is shaped." - Anthony Robbins*

I am grateful for...

1. _____
2. _____
3. _____

Daily affirmations. Mind Candy Voice Note *(Record your affirmations on your smart phone and listen to them several times throughout your day)*

I am... _____

_____

_____

_____

_____

_____

My two massive goals to focus on today:

1. _____
2. _____

Take three deep "oxytocin breaths" by placing your hand
on your heart and exhaling the sound "haaaaa".

My Mind Candy Minute Journal

Date ____/____/_____

"Consumers are statistics. Customers are people." - Stanley Marcus

I am grateful for...

1. _____
2. _____
3. _____

Daily affirmations. Mind Candy Voice Note *(Record your affirmations on your smart phone and listen to them several times throughout your day)*

I am... _____

_____

_____

_____

_____

_____

_____

My two massive goals to focus on today:

1. _____
2. _____

Take three deep "oxytocin breaths" by placing your hand on your heart and exhaling the sound "haaaaa".

My Mind Candy Minute Journal

Date ____/____/_____

"One half of life is luck, the other half is discipline and that's the important half. For without discipline you wouldn't know what to do with luck." - Carl Zuckmeyter

I am grateful for...

1. _____
2. _____
3. _____

Daily affirmations. Mind Candy Voice Note *(Record your affirmations on your smart phone and listen to them several times throughout your day)*

I am... _____

_____
_____
_____
_____
_____
_____

My two massive goals to focus on today:

1. _____
2. _____

Take three deep "oxytocin breaths" by placing your hand on your heart and exhaling the sound "haaaaa".

My Mind Candy Minute Journal

Date ____/____/_____

"Yesterday I dared to struggle. Today I dare to win." - Bernadette Devlin

I am grateful for...

1. _____
2. _____
3. _____

Daily affirmations. Mind Candy Voice Note *(Record your affirmations on your smart phone and listen to them several times throughout your day)*

I am... _____

_____
_____
_____
_____
_____
_____

My two massive goals to focus on today:

1. _____
2. _____

Take three deep "oxytocin breaths" by placing your hand on your heart and exhaling the sound "haaaaa".

My Mind Candy Minute Journal

Date ____/____/_____

"Look at a day when you are supremely satisfied at the end. It's not a day when you lounge around doing nothing. It's when you've had everything to do and you've done it." - Margaret Thatcher

I am grateful for...

1. _____
2. _____
3. _____

Daily affirmations. Mind Candy Voice Note *(Record your affirmations on your smart phone and listen to them several times throughout your day)*

I am... _____

_____
_____
_____
_____
_____
_____

My two massive goals to focus on today:

1. _____
2. _____

Take three deep "oxytocin breaths" by placing your hand on your heart and exhaling the sound "haaaaa".

My Mind Candy Minute Journal

Date ____/____/_____

*"Even if you're on the right track, you'll get run
over if you just sit there." - Will Rogers*

I am grateful for...

1. _____
2. _____
3. _____

Daily affirmations. Mind Candy Voice Note *(Record your affirmations on your smart phone and listen to them several times throughout your day)*

I am... _____

_____

_____

_____

_____

_____

_____

My two massive goals to focus on today:

1. _____
2. _____

Take three deep "oxytocin breaths" by placing your hand
on your heart and exhaling the sound "haaaaa".

My Mind Candy Minute Journal

Date ____/____/_____

"When I was young I observed that nine out of ten things I did were failures, so I did ten times more work." - Bernard Shaw

I am grateful for...

1. _____
2. _____
3. _____

Daily affirmations. Mind Candy Voice Note *(Record your affirmations on your smart phone and listen to them several times throughout your day)*

I am... _____

_____
_____
_____
_____
_____
_____

My two massive goals to focus on today:

1. _____
2. _____

Take three deep "oxytocin breaths" by placing your hand on your heart and exhaling the sound "haaaaa".

My Mind Candy Minute Journal

Date ____/____/_____

"Success is like a ladder and no one has ever climbed a ladder with their hands in their pockets." - Zig Ziglar

I am grateful for...

1. _____
2. _____
3. _____

Daily affirmations. Mind Candy Voice Note *(Record your affirmations on your smart phone and listen to them several times throughout your day)*

I am... _____

_____
_____
_____
_____
_____
_____

My two massive goals to focus on today:

1. _____
2. _____

Take three deep "oxytocin breaths" by placing your hand on your heart and exhaling the sound "haaaaa".

My Mind Candy Minute Journal

Date ____/____/_____

"Nothing can stop the man with the right mental attitude from achieving his goal. Nothing on earth can help the man with the wrong mental attitude." - E. Joseph Cossman

I am grateful for...

1. _____
2. _____
3. _____

Daily affirmations. Mind Candy Voice Note *(Record your affirmations on your smart phone and listen to them several times throughout your day)*

I am... _____

_____
_____
_____
_____
_____
_____

My two massive goals to focus on today:

1. _____
2. _____

Take three deep "oxytocin breaths" by placing your hand on your heart and exhaling the sound "haaaaa".

My Mind Candy Minute Journal

Date ____/____/_____

"I can accept failure but I can't accept not trying." - Michael Jordan

I am grateful for...

1. _____
2. _____
3. _____

Daily affirmations. Mind Candy Voice Note *(Record your affirmations on your smart phone and listen to them several times throughout your day)*

I am... _____
_____
_____
_____
_____
_____

My two massive goals to focus on today:

1. _____
2. _____

Take three deep "oxytocin breaths" by placing your hand
on your heart and exhaling the sound "haaaaa".

My Mind Candy Minute Journal

Date ____/____/_____

"Often the difference between a successful man and a failure is not one's better abilities or ideas, but the courage that one has to bet on his ideas, to take a calculated risk and to act." - Maxwell Maltz

I am grateful for...

1. _____
2. _____
3. _____

Daily affirmations. Mind Candy Voice Note *(Record your affirmations on your smart phone and listen to them several times throughout your day)*

I am... _____
_____
_____
_____
_____
_____
_____

My two massive goals to focus on today:

1. _____
2. _____

Take three deep "oxytocin breaths" by placing your hand on your heart and exhaling the sound "haaaaa".

My Mind Candy Minute Journal

Date ____/____/_____

"Great things are not done by impulse, but by a series of small things brought together." - Vincent van Gogh

I am grateful for...

1. _____
2. _____
3. _____

Daily affirmations. Mind Candy Voice Note *(Record your affirmations on your smart phone and listen to them several times throughout your day)*

I am... _____

_____
_____
_____
_____
_____
_____

My two massive goals to focus on today:

1. _____
2. _____

Take three deep "oxytocin breaths" by placing your hand on your heart and exhaling the sound "haaaaa".

My Mind Candy Minute Journal

Date ____/____/_____

"Picture yourself vividly as winning and that alone will contribute immeasurably to success." - Harry Fosdick

I am grateful for...

1. _____
2. _____
3. _____

Daily affirmations. Mind Candy Voice Note *(Record your affirmations on your smart phone and listen to them several times throughout your day)*

I am... _____

_____
_____
_____
_____
_____
_____

My two massive goals to focus on today:

1. _____
2. _____

Take three deep "oxytocin breaths" by placing your hand on your heart and exhaling the sound "haaaaa".

My Mind Candy Minute Journal

Date ____/____/_____

"Peak performance in life isn't about succeeding all the time or even being happy all the time. It's often about compensating, adjusting, and doing the best you can with what you have right now." - Ken Ravizza

I am grateful for...

1. _____
2. _____
3. _____

Daily affirmations. Mind Candy Voice Note *(Record your affirmations on your smart phone and listen to them several times throughout your day)*

I am... _____

_____
_____
_____
_____
_____
_____

My two massive goals to focus on today:

1. _____
2. _____

Take three deep "oxytocin breaths" by placing your hand on your heart and exhaling the sound "haaaaa".

My Mind Candy Minute Journal

Date ____/____/_____

*"Success is not the result of spontaneous combustion.
You must set yourself on fire." - Reggie Leach*

I am grateful for...

1. _____
2. _____
3. _____

Daily affirmations. Mind Candy Voice Note *(Record your affirmations on your smart phone and listen to them several times throughout your day)*

I am... _____

_____

_____

_____

_____

_____

_____

My two massive goals to focus on today:

1. _____
2. _____

Take three deep "oxytocin breaths" by placing your hand
on your heart and exhaling the sound "haaaaa".

My Mind Candy Minute Journal

Date ____/____/_____

"It doesn't matter what you're trying to accomplish. It's all a matter of discipline. I was determined to discover what life held for me beyond the inner-city streets." - Wilma Rudolph

I am grateful for...

1. _____
2. _____
3. _____

Daily affirmations. Mind Candy Voice Note *(Record your affirmations on your smart phone and listen to them several times throughout your day)*

I am... _____

_____
_____
_____
_____
_____
_____

My two massive goals to focus on today:

1. _____
2. _____

Take three deep "oxytocin breaths" by placing your hand on your heart and exhaling the sound "haaaaa".

My Mind Candy Minute Journal

Date ____/____/_____

"The greatest glory in living lies not in never falling, but in rising every time we fall." - Nelson Mandela

I am grateful for...

1. _____
2. _____
3. _____

Daily affirmations. Mind Candy Voice Note *(Record your affirmations on your smart phone and listen to them several times throughout your day)*

I am... _____

_____
_____
_____
_____
_____
_____

My two massive goals to focus on today:

1. _____
2. _____

Take three deep "oxytocin breaths" by placing your hand on your heart and exhaling the sound "haaaaa".

My Mind Candy Minute Journal

Date ____/____/_____

"A strong successful man is not the victim of his environment. He creates favorable conditions." - Orisen Marden

I am grateful for...

1. _____
2. _____
3. _____

Daily affirmations. Mind Candy Voice Note *(Record your affirmations on your smart phone and listen to them several times throughout your day)*

I am... _____

_____
_____
_____
_____
_____

My two massive goals to focus on today:

1. _____
2. _____

Take three deep "oxytocin breaths" by placing your hand on your heart and exhaling the sound "haaaaa".

My Mind Candy Minute Journal

Date ____/____/_____

"Quality means doing it right when no one is looking." - Henry Ford

I am grateful for...

1. _____
2. _____
3. _____

Daily affirmations. Mind Candy Voice Note *(Record your affirmations on your smart phone and listen to them several times throughout your day)*

I am... _____

_____
_____
_____
_____
_____
_____

My two massive goals to focus on today:

1. _____
2. _____

Take three deep "oxytocin breaths" by placing your hand on your heart and exhaling the sound "haaaaa".

My Mind Candy Minute Journal

Date ____/____/_____

"Dreams are only foolish to those who lack them." - Peter Reese

I am grateful for...

1. _____
2. _____
3. _____

Daily affirmations. Mind Candy Voice Note *(Record your affirmations on your smart phone and listen to them several times throughout your day)*

I am... _____
_____
_____
_____
_____
_____
_____

My two massive goals to focus on today:

1. _____
2. _____

Take three deep "oxytocin breaths" by placing your hand on your heart and exhaling the sound "haaaaa".

My Mind Candy Minute Journal

Date ____/____/_____

"Someday I hope to enjoy enough of what the world calls success so that someone will ask me, 'What's the secret of it?' I shall say simply this: 'I get up when I fall down.'" - Paul Harvey

I am grateful for...

1. _____
2. _____
3. _____

Daily affirmations. Mind Candy Voice Note *(Record your affirmations on your smart phone and listen to them several times throughout your day)*

I am... _____

_____
_____
_____
_____
_____
_____

My two massive goals to focus on today:

1. _____
2. _____

Take three deep "oxytocin breaths" by placing your hand on your heart and exhaling the sound "haaaaa".

My Mind Candy Minute Journal

Date ____/____/_____

"Success of life depends upon keeping one's mind open to opportunity and seizing it when it comes." - Alice Foote MacDougall

I am grateful for...

1. _____
2. _____
3. _____

Daily affirmations. Mind Candy Voice Note *(Record your affirmations on your smart phone and listen to them several times throughout your day)*

I am... _____
_____
_____
_____
_____
_____
_____

My two massive goals to focus on today:

1. _____
2. _____

Take three deep "oxytocin breaths" by placing your hand on your heart and exhaling the sound "haaaaa".

My Mind Candy Minute Journal

Date ____/____/_____

"For true success ask yourself these four questions: Why? Why not? Why not me? Why not now?" - Jimmy Dean

I am grateful for...

1. _____
2. _____
3. _____

Daily affirmations. Mind Candy Voice Note *(Record your affirmations on your smart phone and listen to them several times throughout your day)*

I am... _____
_____
_____
_____
_____
_____
_____

My two massive goals to focus on today:

1. _____
2. _____

Take three deep "oxytocin breaths" by placing your hand on your heart and exhaling the sound "haaaaa".

My Mind Candy Minute Journal

Date ____/____/_____

"Keep away from people who try to belittle your ambition. Small people always do that, but the really great make you feel that you, too, can become great." - Mark Twain

I am grateful for...

1. _____
2. _____
3. _____

Daily affirmations. Mind Candy Voice Note *(Record your affirmations on your smart phone and listen to them several times throughout your day)*

I am... _____

_____
_____
_____
_____
_____
_____

My two massive goals to focus on today:

1. _____
2. _____

Take three deep "oxytocin breaths" by placing your hand on your heart and exhaling the sound "haaaaa".

My Mind Candy Minute Journal

Date ____/____/_____

"Kites rise highest against the wind, not with it." - Winston Churchill

I am grateful for...

1. _____
2. _____
3. _____

Daily affirmations. Mind Candy Voice Note *(Record your affirmations on your smart phone and listen to them several times throughout your day)*

I am... _____
_____
_____
_____
_____
_____
_____

My two massive goals to focus on today:

1. _____
2. _____

Take three deep "oxytocin breaths" by placing your hand on your heart and exhaling the sound "haaaaa".

My Mind Candy Minute Journal

Date ____/____/_____

"Every great man, every successful man, no matter what the field of endeavor, has known the magic that lies in these words: Every adversity has the seed of an equivalent or greater benefit." - W. Clement Stone

I am grateful for...

1. _____
2. _____
3. _____

Daily affirmations. Mind Candy Voice Note *(Record your affirmations on your smart phone and listen to them several times throughout your day)*

I am... _____

_____
_____
_____
_____
_____
_____

My two massive goals to focus on today:

1. _____
2. _____

Take three deep "oxytocin breaths" by placing your hand on your heart and exhaling the sound "haaaaa".

My Mind Candy Minute Journal

Date ____/____/_____

"Success is 10 percent inspiration and 90 percent perspiration." - Thomas Edison

I am grateful for...

1. _____
2. _____
3. _____

Daily affirmations. Mind Candy Voice Note *(Record your affirmations on your smart phone and listen to them several times throughout your day)*

I am... _____
_____
_____
_____
_____
_____
_____

My two massive goals to focus on today:

1. _____
2. _____

Take three deep "oxytocin breaths" by placing your hand on your heart and exhaling the sound "haaaaa".

My Mind Candy Minute Journal

Date ____/____/_____

"Our power is in our ability to decide." - Buckminster Fuller

I am grateful for...

1. _____
2. _____
3. _____

Daily affirmations. Mind Candy Voice Note *(Record your affirmations on your smart phone and listen to them several times throughout your day)*

I am... _____

_____

_____

_____

_____

_____

My two massive goals to focus on today:

1. _____
2. _____

Take three deep "oxytocin breaths" by placing your hand on your heart and exhaling the sound "haaaaa".

My Mind Candy Minute Journal

Date ____/____/_____

"Life affords no higher pleasure than that of surmounting difficulties." - Samuel Johnson

I am grateful for...

1. _____
2. _____
3. _____

Daily affirmations. Mind Candy Voice Note *(Record your affirmations on your smart phone and listen to them several times throughout your day)*

I am... _____

_____
_____
_____
_____
_____
_____

My two massive goals to focus on today:

1. _____
2. _____

Take three deep "oxytocin breaths" by placing your hand on your heart and exhaling the sound "haaaaa".

My Mind Candy Minute Journal

Date ____/____/_____

*"You do not pay the price of success, you enjoy
the price of success." - Zig Ziglar*

I am grateful for...

1. _____
2. _____
3. _____

Daily affirmations. Mind Candy Voice Note *(Record your affirmations on your smart phone and listen to them several times throughout your day)*

I am... _____
_____
_____
_____
_____
_____
_____

My two massive goals to focus on today:

1. _____
2. _____

Take three deep "oxytocin breaths" by placing your hand
on your heart and exhaling the sound "haaaaa".

My Mind Candy Minute Journal

Date ____/____/_____

"Make your life a mission - not an intermission." - Arnold Glasgow

I am grateful for...

1. _____
2. _____
3. _____

Daily affirmations. Mind Candy Voice Note *(Record your affirmations on your smart phone and listen to them several times throughout your day)*

I am... _____

_____
_____
_____
_____
_____
_____

My two massive goals to focus on today:

1. _____
2. _____

Take three deep "oxytocin breaths" by placing your hand
on your heart and exhaling the sound "haaaaa".

My Mind Candy Minute Journal

Date ____/____/_____

"Do it trembling if you must, but do it!" - Emmet Fox

I am grateful for...

1. _____
2. _____
3. _____

Daily affirmations. Mind Candy Voice Note *(Record your affirmations on your smart phone and listen to them several times throughout your day)*

I am... _____
_____
_____
_____
_____
_____
_____

My two massive goals to focus on today:

1. _____
2. _____

Take three deep "oxytocin breaths" by placing your hand
on your heart and exhaling the sound "haaaaa".

My Mind Candy Minute Journal

Date ____/____/_____

"Consider the postage stamp. It secures success through its ability to stick to one thing until it gets there." - Josh Billings

I am grateful for...

1. _____
2. _____
3. _____

Daily affirmations. Mind Candy Voice Note *(Record your affirmations on your smart phone and listen to them several times throughout your day)*

I am... _____

_____

_____

_____

_____

_____

My two massive goals to focus on today:

1. _____
2. _____

Take three deep "oxytocin breaths" by placing your hand on your heart and exhaling the sound "haaaaa".

My Mind Candy Minute Journal

Date ____/____/_____

"It takes twenty years to become an overnight success." - Eddie Cantor

I am grateful for...

1. _____
2. _____
3. _____

Daily affirmations. Mind Candy Voice Note *(Record your affirmations on your smart phone and listen to them several times throughout your day)*

I am... _____

_____
_____
_____
_____
_____
_____

My two massive goals to focus on today:

1. _____
2. _____

Take three deep "oxytocin breaths" by placing your hand on your heart and exhaling the sound "haaaaa".

My Mind Candy Minute Journal

Date ____/____/_____

"The basic rule of free enterprise: You must give in order to get." - Scott Alexander

I am grateful for...

1. _____
2. _____
3. _____

Daily affirmations. Mind Candy Voice Note *(Record your affirmations on your smart phone and listen to them several times throughout your day)*

I am... _____

_____
_____
_____
_____
_____

My two massive goals to focus on today:

1. _____
2. _____

Take three deep "oxytocin breaths" by placing your hand on your heart and exhaling the sound "haaaaa".

My Mind Candy Minute Journal

Date ____/____/_____

"The more tranquil a man becomes, the greater is his success, his influence, his power for good. Calmness of mind is one of the beautiful jewels of wisdom." - James Allen

I am grateful for...

1. _____
2. _____
3. _____

Daily affirmations. Mind Candy Voice Note *(Record your affirmations on your smart phone and listen to them several times throughout your day)*

I am... _____

_____
_____
_____
_____
_____
_____

My two massive goals to focus on today:

1. _____
2. _____

Take three deep "oxytocin breaths" by placing your hand on your heart and exhaling the sound "haaaaa".

My Mind Candy Minute Journal

Date ____/____/_____

"The thing always happens that you really believe in and the belief in a thing makes it happen." - Frank Lloyd Wright

I am grateful for...

1. _____
2. _____
3. _____

Daily affirmations. Mind Candy Voice Note *(Record your affirmations on your smart phone and listen to them several times throughout your day)*

I am... _____

_____
_____
_____
_____
_____
_____

My two massive goals to focus on today:

1. _____
2. _____

Take three deep "oxytocin breaths" by placing your hand on your heart and exhaling the sound "haaaaa".

My Mind Candy Minute Journal

Date ____/____/_____

"The road to success is always under construction." - Lily Tomlin

I am grateful for...

1. _____
2. _____
3. _____

Daily affirmations. Mind Candy Voice Note *(Record your affirmations on your smart phone and listen to them several times throughout your day)*

I am... _____

_____

_____

_____

_____

_____

_____

My two massive goals to focus on today:

1. _____
2. _____

Take three deep "oxytocin breaths" by placing your hand on your heart and exhaling the sound "haaaaa".

My Mind Candy Minute Journal

Date ____/____/_____

"Hope is not a dream, but a way of making dreams become reality." - L.J. Cardina Suenens

I am grateful for...

1. _____
2. _____
3. _____

Daily affirmations. Mind Candy Voice Note *(Record your affirmations on your smart phone and listen to them several times throughout your day)*

I am... _____

_____

_____

_____

_____

_____

_____

My two massive goals to focus on today:

1. _____
2. _____

Take three deep "oxytocin breaths" by placing your hand on your heart and exhaling the sound "haaaaa".

My Mind Candy Minute Journal

Date ____/____/_____

"They can because they think they can." - Virgil

I am grateful for...

1. _____
2. _____
3. _____

Daily affirmations. Mind Candy Voice Note *(Record your affirmations on your smart phone and listen to them several times throughout your day)*

I am... _____

_____
_____
_____
_____
_____
_____

My two massive goals to focus on today:

1. _____
2. _____

Take three deep "oxytocin breaths" by placing your hand on your heart and exhaling the sound "haaaaa".

My Mind Candy Minute Journal

Date ____/____/_____

"We are made to persist. That's how we find out who we are." - Tobias Wolff

I am grateful for...

1. _____
2. _____
3. _____

Daily affirmations. Mind Candy Voice Note *(Record your affirmations on your smart phone and listen to them several times throughout your day)*

I am... _____

_____

_____

_____

_____

_____

_____

My two massive goals to focus on today:

1. _____
2. _____

Take three deep "oxytocin breaths" by placing your hand on your heart and exhaling the sound "haaaaa".

My Mind Candy Minute Journal

Date ____/____/_____

"Success has nothing to do with what you gain in life or accomplish for yourself. It's what you do for others." - Danny Thomas

I am grateful for...

1. _____
2. _____
3. _____

Daily affirmations. Mind Candy Voice Note *(Record your affirmations on your smart phone and listen to them several times throughout your day)*

I am... _____

_____
_____
_____
_____
_____
_____

My two massive goals to focus on today:

1. _____
2. _____

Take three deep "oxytocin breaths" by placing your hand on your heart and exhaling the sound "haaaaa".

My Mind Candy Minute Journal

Date _____/_____/_____

"Men are born to succeed, not to fail." - Henry David Thoreau

I am grateful for...

1. _____
2. _____
3. _____

Daily affirmations. Mind Candy Voice Note *(Record your affirmations on your smart phone and listen to them several times throughout your day)*

I am... _____

_____

_____

_____

_____

_____

_____

My two massive goals to focus on today:

1. _____
2. _____

Take three deep "oxytocin breaths" by placing your hand on your heart and exhaling the sound "haaaaa".

My Mind Candy Minute Journal

Date ____/____/_____

"It's no use saying, 'We are doing our best.' You have got to succeed in doing what is necessary." - Winston Churchill

I am grateful for...

1. _____
2. _____
3. _____

Daily affirmations. Mind Candy Voice Note *(Record your affirmations on your smart phone and listen to them several times throughout your day)*

I am... _____
_____
_____
_____
_____
_____
_____

My two massive goals to focus on today:

1. _____
2. _____

Take three deep "oxytocin breaths" by placing your hand on your heart and exhaling the sound "haaaaa".

My Mind Candy Minute Journal

Date ____/____/_____

"Success is a process, a quality of mind and way of being, an outgoing affirmation of life." - Alex Noble

I am grateful for...

1. _____
2. _____
3. _____

Daily affirmations. Mind Candy Voice Note *(Record your affirmations on your smart phone and listen to them several times throughout your day)*

I am... _____

_____
_____
_____
_____
_____
_____

My two massive goals to focus on today:

1. _____
2. _____

Take three deep "oxytocin breaths" by placing your hand on your heart and exhaling the sound "haaaaa".

My Mind Candy Minute Journal

Date ____/____/_____

"Only those who will risk going too far can possibly find out how far they can go." - T.S. Eliot

I am grateful for...

1. _____
2. _____
3. _____

Daily affirmations. Mind Candy Voice Note *(Record your affirmations on your smart phone and listen to them several times throughout your day)*

I am... _____

_____
_____
_____
_____
_____
_____

My two massive goals to focus on today:

1. _____
2. _____

Take three deep "oxytocin breaths" by placing your hand on your heart and exhaling the sound "haaaaa".

My Mind Candy Minute Journal

Date ____/____/_____

"A man can succeed at almost anything for which he has unlimited enthusiasm." - Charles Schwab

I am grateful for...

1. _____
2. _____
3. _____

Daily affirmations. Mind Candy Voice Note *(Record your affirmations on your smart phone and listen to them several times throughout your day)*

I am... _____

_____
_____
_____
_____
_____
_____

My two massive goals to focus on today:

1. _____
2. _____

Take three deep "oxytocin breaths" by placing your hand on your heart and exhaling the sound "haaaaa".

My Mind Candy Minute Journal

Date ____/____/_____

"The five essential entrepreneurial skills for success: Concentration, Discrimination, Organization, Innovation and Communication." - Michael Gerber

I am grateful for...

1. _____
2. _____
3. _____

Daily affirmations. Mind Candy Voice Note *(Record your affirmations on your smart phone and listen to them several times throughout your day)*

I am... _____

_____
_____
_____
_____
_____
_____

My two massive goals to focus on today:

1. _____
2. _____

Take three deep "oxytocin breaths" by placing your hand on your heart and exhaling the sound "haaaaa".

My Mind Candy Minute Journal

Date ____/____/_____

"One sound idea is all that you need to achieve success." - Napoleon Hill

I am grateful for...

1. _____
2. _____
3. _____

Daily affirmations. Mind Candy Voice Note *(Record your affirmations on your smart phone and listen to them several times throughout your day)*

I am... _____

_____
_____
_____
_____
_____
_____

My two massive goals to focus on today:

1. _____
2. _____

Take three deep "oxytocin breaths" by placing your hand on your heart and exhaling the sound "haaaaa".

My Mind Candy Minute Journal

Date ____/____/_____

"We can do anything we want to do if we stick to it long enough." - Helen Keller

I am grateful for...

1. _____
2. _____
3. _____

Daily affirmations. Mind Candy Voice Note *(Record your affirmations on your smart phone and listen to them several times throughout your day)*

I am... _____

_____
_____
_____
_____
_____
_____

My two massive goals to focus on today:

1. _____
2. _____

Take three deep "oxytocin breaths" by placing your hand on your heart and exhaling the sound "haaaaa".

My Mind Candy Minute Journal

Date ____/____/_____

"Success seems to be largely a matter of hanging on after others have let go." - William Feather

I am grateful for...

1. _____
2. _____
3. _____

Daily affirmations. Mind Candy Voice Note *(Record your affirmations on your smart phone and listen to them several times throughout your day)*

I am... _____

_____

_____

_____

_____

_____

My two massive goals to focus on today:

1. _____
2. _____

Take three deep "oxytocin breaths" by placing your hand on your heart and exhaling the sound "haaaaa".

My Mind Candy Minute Journal

Date ____/____/_____

"Hard work is the price we must pay for success. I think you can accomplish anything if you're willing to pay the price." - Vince Lombardi

I am grateful for...

1. _____
2. _____
3. _____

Daily affirmations. Mind Candy Voice Note *(Record your affirmations on your smart phone and listen to them several times throughout your day)*

I am... _____
_____
_____
_____
_____
_____
_____

My two massive goals to focus on today:

1. _____
2. _____

Take three deep "oxytocin breaths" by placing your hand on your heart and exhaling the sound "haaaaa".

My Mind Candy Minute Journal

Date ____/____/_____

"Failure is only the opportunity to begin again more intelligently." - Henry Ford

I am grateful for...

1. _____
2. _____
3. _____

Daily affirmations. Mind Candy Voice Note *(Record your affirmations on your smart phone and listen to them several times throughout your day)*

I am... _____

_____

_____

_____

_____

_____

_____

My two massive goals to focus on today:

1. _____
2. _____

Take three deep "oxytocin breaths" by placing your hand on your heart and exhaling the sound "haaaaa".

My Mind Candy Minute Journal

Date ____/____/_____

*"If you have no critics you'll likely have
no success." - Malcolm Forbes*

I am grateful for...

1. _____
2. _____
3. _____

Daily affirmations. Mind Candy Voice Note *(Record your affirmations on your smart phone and listen to them several times throughout your day)*

I am... _____

_____
_____
_____
_____
_____
_____

My two massive goals to focus on today:

1. _____
2. _____

Take three deep "oxytocin breaths" by placing your hand
on your heart and exhaling the sound "haaaaa".

My Mind Candy Minute Journal

Date ____/____/_____

"In the middle of difficulty, lies opportunity." - Albert Einstein

I am grateful for...

1. _____
2. _____
3. _____

Daily affirmations. Mind Candy Voice Note *(Record your affirmations on your smart phone and listen to them several times throughout your day)*

I am... _____

_____
_____
_____
_____
_____
_____

My two massive goals to focus on today:

1. _____
2. _____

Take three deep "oxytocin breaths" by placing your hand on your heart and exhaling the sound "haaaaa".

My Mind Candy Minute Journal

Date ____/____/_____

"If you want to be successful, it's just this simple: Know what you are doing, love what you are doing, and believe in what you are doing." - Will Rogers

I am grateful for...

1. _____
2. _____
3. _____

Daily affirmations. Mind Candy Voice Note *(Record your affirmations on your smart phone and listen to them several times throughout your day)*

I am... _____

_____
_____
_____
_____
_____
_____

My two massive goals to focus on today:

1. _____
2. _____

Take three deep "oxytocin breaths" by placing your hand on your heart and exhaling the sound "haaaaa".

My Mind Candy Minute Journal

Date ____/____/_____

"Human beings can alter their lives by altering their attitudes of mind." - William James

I am grateful for...

1. _____
2. _____
3. _____

Daily affirmations. Mind Candy Voice Note *(Record your affirmations on your smart phone and listen to them several times throughout your day)*

I am... _____

_____
_____
_____
_____
_____
_____

My two massive goals to focus on today:

1. _____
2. _____

Take three deep "oxytocin breaths" by placing your hand on your heart and exhaling the sound "haaaaa".

My Mind Candy Minute Journal

Date ____/____/_____

"Give me a stock clerk with a goal and I'll give you a man who will make history. Give me a man with no goals and I'll give you a stock clerk." - J.C. Penney

I am grateful for...

1. _____
2. _____
3. _____

Daily affirmations. Mind Candy Voice Note *(Record your affirmations on your smart phone and listen to them several times throughout your day)*

I am... _____

_____
_____
_____
_____
_____
_____

My two massive goals to focus on today:

1. _____
2. _____

Take three deep "oxytocin breaths" by placing your hand on your heart and exhaling the sound "haaaaa".

My Mind Candy Minute Journal

Date ____/____/_____

*"The successful man is one who had the
chance and took it." - Roger Babson*

I am grateful for...

1. _____
2. _____
3. _____

Daily affirmations. Mind Candy Voice Note *(Record your affirmations on your smart phone and listen to them several times throughout your day)*

I am... _____

_____
_____
_____
_____
_____
_____

My two massive goals to focus on today:

1. _____
2. _____

Take three deep "oxytocin breaths" by placing your hand
on your heart and exhaling the sound "haaaaa".

My Mind Candy Minute Journal

Date ____/____/_____

*"Make the most of yourself, for that is all there
is for you." - Ralph Waldo Emerson*

I am grateful for...

1. _____
2. _____
3. _____

Daily affirmations. Mind Candy Voice Note *(Record your affirmations on your smart phone and listen to them several times throughout your day)*

I am... _____

_____
_____
_____
_____
_____
_____

My two massive goals to focus on today:

1. _____
2. _____

Take three deep "oxytocin breaths" by placing your hand
on your heart and exhaling the sound "haaaaa".

My Mind Candy Minute Journal

Date ____/____/_____

"If you are never scared, embarrassed or hurt, it means you never take chances." - Julia Soul

I am grateful for...

1. _____
2. _____
3. _____

Daily affirmations. Mind Candy Voice Note *(Record your affirmations on your smart phone and listen to them several times throughout your day)*

I am... _____

_____
_____
_____
_____
_____
_____

My two massive goals to focus on today:

1. _____
2. _____

Take three deep "oxytocin breaths" by placing your hand on your heart and exhaling the sound "haaaaa".

My Mind Candy Minute Journal

Date _____/_____/_____

"Man is a goal-seeking animal. His life only has meaning if he is reaching out and striving for his goals." - Aristotle

I am grateful for...

1. _____
2. _____
3. _____

Daily affirmations. Mind Candy Voice Note *(Record your affirmations on your smart phone and listen to them several times throughout your day)*

I am... _____

_____
_____
_____
_____
_____
_____

My two massive goals to focus on today:

1. _____
2. _____

Take three deep "oxytocin breaths" by placing your hand on your heart and exhaling the sound "haaaaa".

My Mind Candy Minute Journal

Date ____/____/_____

"The first step towards success in any occupation is to become interested in it." - Sir William Osler

I am grateful for...

1. _____
2. _____
3. _____

Daily affirmations. Mind Candy Voice Note *(Record your affirmations on your smart phone and listen to them several times throughout your day)*

I am... _____

_____

_____

_____

_____

_____

_____

My two massive goals to focus on today:

1. _____
2. _____

Take three deep "oxytocin breaths" by placing your hand on your heart and exhaling the sound "haaaaa".

My Mind Candy Minute Journal

Date ____/____/_____

"Every man is free to rise as far as he's able or willing, but the degree to which he thinks determines the degree to which he'll rise." - Ayn Rand

I am grateful for...

1. _____
2. _____
3. _____

Daily affirmations. Mind Candy Voice Note *(Record your affirmations on your smart phone and listen to them several times throughout your day)*

I am... _____

_____
_____
_____
_____
_____
_____

My two massive goals to focus on today:

1. _____
2. _____

Take three deep "oxytocin breaths" by placing your hand on your heart and exhaling the sound "haaaaa".

My Mind Candy Minute Journal

Date _____/_____/_____

"The successful person places more attention on doing the right thing rather than doing things right." - Peter Drucker

I am grateful for...

1. _____
2. _____
3. _____

Daily affirmations. Mind Candy Voice Note *(Record your affirmations on your smart phone and listen to them several times throughout your day)*

I am... _____

_____
_____
_____
_____
_____
_____

My two massive goals to focus on today:

1. _____
2. _____

Take three deep "oxytocin breaths" by placing your hand on your heart and exhaling the sound "haaaaa".

My Mind Candy Minute Journal

Date ____/____/_____

"I have failed over and over again - that is why I succeed." - Michael Jordan

I am grateful for...

1. _____
2. _____
3. _____

Daily affirmations. Mind Candy Voice Note *(Record your affirmations on your smart phone and listen to them several times throughout your day)*

I am... _____

_____
_____
_____
_____
_____
_____

My two massive goals to focus on today:

1. _____
2. _____

Take three deep "oxytocin breaths" by placing your hand on your heart and exhaling the sound "haaaaa".

My Mind Candy Minute Journal

Date ____/____/_____

"The great end of life is not knowledge but action." - Thomas Henry Huxley

I am grateful for...

1. _____
2. _____
3. _____

Daily affirmations. Mind Candy Voice Note *(Record your affirmations on your smart phone and listen to them several times throughout your day)*

I am... _____

_____
_____
_____
_____
_____
_____

My two massive goals to focus on today:

1. _____
2. _____

Take three deep "oxytocin breaths" by placing your hand on your heart and exhaling the sound "haaaaa".

My Mind Candy Minute Journal

Date ____/____/_____

"The men who have done big things are those who were not afraid to attempt big things, who were not afraid to risk failure in order to gain success." - B.C. Forbes

I am grateful for...

1. _____
2. _____
3. _____

Daily affirmations. Mind Candy Voice Note *(Record your affirmations on your smart phone and listen to them several times throughout your day)*

I am... _____

_____
_____
_____
_____
_____
_____
_____

My two massive goals to focus on today:

1. _____
2. _____

Take three deep "oxytocin breaths" by placing your hand on your heart and exhaling the sound "haaaaa".

My Mind Candy Minute Journal

Date ____/____/_____

*"Do not let what you cannot do interfere with
what you can do." - John Wooden*

I am grateful for...

1. _____
2. _____
3. _____

Daily affirmations. Mind Candy Voice Note *(Record your affirmations on your smart phone and listen to them several times throughout your day)*

I am... _____

_____
_____
_____
_____
_____

My two massive goals to focus on today:

1. _____
2. _____

Take three deep "oxytocin breaths" by placing your hand
on your heart and exhaling the sound "haaaaa".

My Mind Candy Minute Journal

Date ____/____/_____

"Success is living up to your potential. That's all. Wake up with a smile and go after life ... live it, enjoy it, taste it, smell it, feel it." - Joe Knapp

I am grateful for...

1. _____
2. _____
3. _____

Daily affirmations. Mind Candy Voice Note *(Record your affirmations on your smart phone and listen to them several times throughout your day)*

I am... _____
_____
_____
_____
_____
_____
_____

My two massive goals to focus on today:

1. _____
2. _____

Take three deep "oxytocin breaths" by placing your hand on your heart and exhaling the sound "haaaaa".

My Mind Candy Minute Journal

Date ____/____/_____

"Only those who dare to fail greatly can ever achieve greatly." - Robert F. Kennedy

I am grateful for...

1. _____
2. _____
3. _____

Daily affirmations. Mind Candy Voice Note *(Record your affirmations on your smart phone and listen to them several times throughout your day)*

I am... _____

_____

_____

_____

_____

_____

My two massive goals to focus on today:

1. _____
2. _____

Take three deep "oxytocin breaths" by placing your hand on your heart and exhaling the sound "haaaaa".

My Mind Candy Minute Journal

Date _____/_____/_____

"A leader has the vision and conviction that a dream can be achieved. He inspired the power and energy to get it done." - Ralph Lauren

I am grateful for...

1. _____
2. _____
3. _____

Daily affirmations. Mind Candy Voice Note *(Record your affirmations on your smart phone and listen to them several times throughout your day)*

I am... _____

_____
_____
_____
_____
_____
_____

My two massive goals to focus on today:

1. _____
2. _____

Take three deep "oxytocin breaths" by placing your hand on your heart and exhaling the sound "haaaaa".

My Mind Candy Minute Journal

Date ____/____/_____

*"What the mind can conceive and believe, the
mind can achieve." - Napoleon Hill*

I am grateful for...

1. _____
2. _____
3. _____

Daily affirmations. Mind Candy Voice Note *(Record your affirmations on your smart phone and listen to them several times throughout your day)*

I am... _____

_____
_____
_____
_____
_____
_____

My two massive goals to focus on today:

1. _____
2. _____

Take three deep "oxytocin breaths" by placing your hand
on your heart and exhaling the sound "haaaaa".

My Mind Candy Minute Journal

Date ____/____/_____

"The way to succeed is to double your failure rate. Failure is the opportunity to begin again more intelligently." - Henry Ford

I am grateful for...

1. _____
2. _____
3. _____

Daily affirmations. Mind Candy Voice Note *(Record your affirmations on your smart phone and listen to them several times throughout your day)*

I am...   _____
_____
_____
_____
_____
_____
_____

My two massive goals to focus on today:

1. _____
2. _____

Take three deep "oxytocin breaths" by placing your hand on your heart and exhaling the sound "haaaaa".

My Mind Candy Minute Journal

Date ____/____/_____

"Sooner or later those who win are those who think they can." - Richard Bach

I am grateful for...

1. _____
2. _____
3. _____

Daily affirmations. Mind Candy Voice Note *(Record your affirmations on your smart phone and listen to them several times throughout your day)*

I am... _____

_____
_____
_____
_____
_____

My two massive goals to focus on today:

1. _____
2. _____

Take three deep "oxytocin breaths" by placing your hand on your heart and exhaling the sound "haaaaa".

My Mind Candy Minute Journal

Date ____/____/_____

"People become really quite remarkable when they start thinking that they can do things. When they believe in themselves they have the first secret of success." - Norman Vincent Peale

I am grateful for...

1. _____
2. _____
3. _____

Daily affirmations. Mind Candy Voice Note *(Record your affirmations on your smart phone and listen to them several times throughout your day)*

I am... _____

_____

_____

_____

_____

_____

_____

My two massive goals to focus on today:

1. _____
2. _____

Take three deep "oxytocin breaths" by placing your hand on your heart and exhaling the sound "haaaaa".

My Mind Candy Minute Journal

Date ____/____/_____

"Spectacular achievements are always preceded by painstaking preparation." - Roger Staubach

I am grateful for...

1. _____
2. _____
3. _____

Daily affirmations. Mind Candy Voice Note *(Record your affirmations on your smart phone and listen to them several times throughout your day)*

I am... _____

_____
_____
_____
_____
_____
_____

My two massive goals to focus on today:

1. _____
2. _____

Take three deep "oxytocin breaths" by placing your hand on your heart and exhaling the sound "haaaaa".

My Mind Candy Minute Journal

Date ____/____/_____

"If we did all the things we are capable of doing, we would literally astonish ourselves." - Thomas Edison

I am grateful for...

1. _____
2. _____
3. _____

Daily affirmations. Mind Candy Voice Note *(Record your affirmations on your smart phone and listen to them several times throughout your day)*

I am... _____

_____
_____
_____
_____
_____
_____

My two massive goals to focus on today:

1. _____
2. _____

Take three deep "oxytocin breaths" by placing your hand on your heart and exhaling the sound "haaaaa".

My Mind Candy Minute Journal

Date ____/____/_____

"The journey of a thousand miles begins with one step." - Lao-Tse

I am grateful for...

1. _____
2. _____
3. _____

Daily affirmations. Mind Candy Voice Note *(Record your affirmations on your smart phone and listen to them several times throughout your day)*

I am... _____

_____
_____
_____
_____
_____
_____

My two massive goals to focus on today:

1. _____
2. _____

Take three deep "oxytocin breaths" by placing your hand
on your heart and exhaling the sound "haaaaa".

My Mind Candy Minute Journal

Date _____/_____/_____

"Success is the maximum utilization of the ability that you have." - Zig Ziglar

I am grateful for...

1. _____
2. _____
3. _____

Daily affirmations. Mind Candy Voice Note *(Record your affirmations on your smart phone and listen to them several times throughout your day)*

I am... _____

_____
_____
_____
_____
_____
_____

My two massive goals to focus on today:

1. _____
2. _____

Take three deep "oxytocin breaths" by placing your hand on your heart and exhaling the sound "haaaaa".

My Mind Candy Minute Journal

Date ____/____/_____

"The difficulties and struggles of today are but the price we must pay for the accomplishments and victories of tomorrow." - William Boetcker

I am grateful for...

1. _____
2. _____
3. _____

Daily affirmations. Mind Candy Voice Note *(Record your affirmations on your smart phone and listen to them several times throughout your day)*

I am... _____

_____
_____
_____
_____
_____
_____

My two massive goals to focus on today:

1. _____
2. _____

Take three deep "oxytocin breaths" by placing your hand on your heart and exhaling the sound "haaaaa".

My Mind Candy Minute Journal

Date ____/____/_____

"Do what you can with what you have where you are." - Theodore Roosevelt

I am grateful for...

1. _____
2. _____
3. _____

Daily affirmations. Mind Candy Voice Note *(Record your affirmations on your smart phone and listen to them several times throughout your day)*

I am... _____
_____
_____
_____
_____
_____
_____

My two massive goals to focus on today:

1. _____
2. _____

Take three deep "oxytocin breaths" by placing your hand on your heart and exhaling the sound "haaaaa".

My Mind Candy Minute Journal

Date ____/____/_____

"Failure is the tuition you pay for success." - Walter Brunell

I am grateful for...

1. _____
2. _____
3. _____

Daily affirmations. Mind Candy Voice Note *(Record your affirmations on your smart phone and listen to them several times throughout your day)*

I am... _____

_____
_____
_____
_____
_____
_____

My two massive goals to focus on today:

1. _____
2. _____

Take three deep "oxytocin breaths" by placing your hand on your heart and exhaling the sound "haaaaa".

My Mind Candy Minute Journal

Date _____/_____/_____

"Real wealth equals ideas plus energy." - Buckminster Fuller

I am grateful for...

1. _____
2. _____
3. _____

Daily affirmations. Mind Candy Voice Note *(Record your affirmations on your smart phone and listen to them several times throughout your day)*

I am... _____
_____
_____
_____
_____
_____
_____

My two massive goals to focus on today:

1. _____
2. _____

Take three deep "oxytocin breaths" by placing your hand
on your heart and exhaling the sound "haaaaa".

My Mind Candy Minute Journal

Date ____/____/_____

"We grow great by dreams. All big men are dreamers." - Woodrow Wilson

I am grateful for...

1. _____
2. _____
3. _____

Daily affirmations. Mind Candy Voice Note *(Record your affirmations on your smart phone and listen to them several times throughout your day)*

I am... _____

_____
_____
_____
_____
_____
_____

My two massive goals to focus on today:

1. _____
2. _____

Take three deep "oxytocin breaths" by placing your hand on your heart and exhaling the sound "haaaaa".

My Mind Candy Minute Journal

Date ____/____/_____

"We are continually faced by great opportunities brilliantly disguised as insoluble problems." - Lee Iococca

I am grateful for...

1. _____
2. _____
3. _____

Daily affirmations. Mind Candy Voice Note *(Record your affirmations on your smart phone and listen to them several times throughout your day)*

I am... _____
_____
_____
_____
_____
_____
_____

My two massive goals to focus on today:

1. _____
2. _____

Take three deep "oxytocin breaths" by placing your hand on your heart and exhaling the sound "haaaaa".

My Mind Candy Minute Journal

Date ____/____/_____

"Private victories precede public victories." - Stephen R. Covey

I am grateful for...

1. _____
2. _____
3. _____

Daily affirmations. Mind Candy Voice Note *(Record your affirmations on your smart phone and listen to them several times throughout your day)*

I am... _____

_____

_____

_____

_____

_____

_____

My two massive goals to focus on today:

1. _____
2. _____

Take three deep "oxytocin breaths" by placing your hand
on your heart and exhaling the sound "haaaaa".

My Mind Candy Minute Journal

Date _____/_____/_____

"Great minds have purpose, others have wishes." - Washington Irving

I am grateful for...

1. _____
2. _____
3. _____

Daily affirmations. Mind Candy Voice Note *(Record your affirmations on your smart phone and listen to them several times throughout your day)*

I am... _____

_____
_____
_____
_____
_____

My two massive goals to focus on today:

1. _____
2. _____

Take three deep "oxytocin breaths" by placing your hand on your heart and exhaling the sound "haaaaa".

My Mind Candy Minute Journal

Date ____/____/_____

"The common denominator of success is in forming the habit of doing the things that failures don't like to do." - Albert Gray

I am grateful for...

1. _____
2. _____
3. _____

Daily affirmations. Mind Candy Voice Note *(Record your affirmations on your smart phone and listen to them several times throughout your day)*

I am... _____

_____
_____
_____
_____
_____
_____
_____

My two massive goals to focus on today:

1. _____
2. _____

Take three deep "oxytocin breaths" by placing your hand on your heart and exhaling the sound "haaaaa".

My Mind Candy Minute Journal

Date ____/____/_____

"Singleness of purpose is one of the chief essentials for success in life, no matter what may be one's aim." - John D. Rockefeller

I am grateful for...

1. _____
2. _____
3. _____

Daily affirmations. Mind Candy Voice Note *(Record your affirmations on your smart phone and listen to them several times throughout your day)*

I am... _____

_____
_____
_____
_____
_____
_____

My two massive goals to focus on today:

1. _____
2. _____

Take three deep "oxytocin breaths" by placing your hand on your heart and exhaling the sound "haaaaa".

My Mind Candy Minute Journal

Date ____/____/_____

"I will say this about being an optimist: even when things don't turn out well, you are certain they will get better." - Frank Hughes

I am grateful for...

1. _____
2. _____
3. _____

Daily affirmations. Mind Candy Voice Note *(Record your affirmations on your smart phone and listen to them several times throughout your day)*

I am... _____

_____

_____

_____

_____

_____

_____

My two massive goals to focus on today:

1. _____
2. _____

Take three deep "oxytocin breaths" by placing your hand on your heart and exhaling the sound "haaaaa".

My Mind Candy Minute Journal

Date _____/_____/_____

"Some men see things as they are, and say, 'Why?' I dream of things that never were, and say, 'Why not?'" - George Bernard Shaw

I am grateful for...

1. _____
2. _____
3. _____

Daily affirmations. Mind Candy Voice Note *(Record your affirmations on your smart phone and listen to them several times throughout your day)*

I am... _____

_____
_____
_____
_____
_____
_____

My two massive goals to focus on today:

1. _____
2. _____

Take three deep "oxytocin breaths" by placing your hand on your heart and exhaling the sound "haaaaa".

My Mind Candy Minute Journal

Date ____/____/_____

*"Perseverance is a great element of success." -
Henry Wadsworth Longfellow*

I am grateful for...

1. _____
2. _____
3. _____

Daily affirmations. Mind Candy Voice Note *(Record your affirmations on your smart phone and listen to them several times throughout your day)*

I am... _____
_____
_____
_____
_____
_____
_____

My two massive goals to focus on today:

1. _____
2. _____

Take three deep "oxytocin breaths" by placing your hand
on your heart and exhaling the sound "haaaaa".

My Mind Candy Minute Journal

Date ____/____/_____

"The only limit to our realization of tomorrow will be our doubts of today." - Franklin D. Roosevelt

I am grateful for...

1. _____
2. _____
3. _____

Daily affirmations. Mind Candy Voice Note *(Record your affirmations on your smart phone and listen to them several times throughout your day)*

I am... _____

_____
_____
_____
_____
_____

My two massive goals to focus on today:

1. _____
2. _____

Take three deep "oxytocin breaths" by placing your hand on your heart and exhaling the sound "haaaaa".

My Mind Candy Minute Journal

Date ____/____/_____

"A person's way of doing things is the direct result of the way he thinks about things." - Wallace D. Wattles

I am grateful for...

1. _____
2. _____
3. _____

Daily affirmations. Mind Candy Voice Note *(Record your affirmations on your smart phone and listen to them several times throughout your day)*

I am... _____

_____
_____
_____
_____
_____
_____

My two massive goals to focus on today:

1. _____
2. _____

Take three deep "oxytocin breaths" by placing your hand on your heart and exhaling the sound "haaaaa".

My Mind Candy Minute Journal

Date _____/_____/_____

"Success demands singleness of purpose." - Vince Lombardi

I am grateful for...

1. _____
2. _____
3. _____

Daily affirmations. Mind Candy Voice Note *(Record your affirmations on your smart phone and listen to them several times throughout your day)*

I am... _____

_____

_____

_____

_____

_____

_____

My two massive goals to focus on today:

1. _____
2. _____

Take three deep "oxytocin breaths" by placing your hand on your heart and exhaling the sound "haaaaa".

My Mind Candy Minute Journal

Date ____/____/_____

"A man is but of product of his thought, What he thinks he becomes." - Mahatma Gandhi

I am grateful for...

1. _____
2. _____
3. _____

Daily affirmations. Mind Candy Voice Note *(Record your affirmations on your smart phone and listen to them several times throughout your day)*

I am... _____

_____
_____
_____
_____
_____
_____

My two massive goals to focus on today:

1. _____
2. _____

Take three deep "oxytocin breaths" by placing your hand on your heart and exhaling the sound "haaaaa".

My Mind Candy Minute Journal

Date _____/_____/_____

"The secret of success is learning how to use pain and pleasure instead of having pain and pleasure use you. If you do that, you're in control of your life. If you don't, life controls you." - Anthony Robbins

I am grateful for...

1. _____
2. _____
3. _____

Daily affirmations. Mind Candy Voice Note *(Record your affirmations on your smart phone and listen to them several times throughout your day)*

I am... _____

_____
_____
_____
_____
_____
_____

My two massive goals to focus on today:

1. _____
2. _____

Take three deep "oxytocin breaths" by placing your hand on your heart and exhaling the sound "haaaaa".

My Mind Candy Minute Journal

Date ____/____/_____

"First, say to yourself what you would be, then do what you have to do." - Epictetus

I am grateful for...

1. _____
2. _____
3. _____

Daily affirmations. Mind Candy Voice Note *(Record your affirmations on your smart phone and listen to them several times throughout your day)*

I am... _____

_____
_____
_____
_____
_____
_____

My two massive goals to focus on today:

1. _____
2. _____

Take three deep "oxytocin breaths" by placing your hand on your heart and exhaling the sound "haaaaa".

My Mind Candy Minute Journal

Date ____/____/_____

"If you can dream it, you can do it. Your limits are all within yourself." - Brian Tracy

I am grateful for...

1. _____
2. _____
3. _____

Daily affirmations. Mind Candy Voice Note *(Record your affirmations on your smart phone and listen to them several times throughout your day)*

I am... _____

_____
_____
_____
_____
_____
_____

My two massive goals to focus on today:

1. _____
2. _____

Take three deep "oxytocin breaths" by placing your hand on your heart and exhaling the sound "haaaaa".

My Mind Candy Minute Journal

Date ____/____/_____

"A problem is a chance for you to do your best." - Duke Ellington

I am grateful for...

1. _____
2. _____
3. _____

Daily affirmations. Mind Candy Voice Note *(Record your affirmations on your smart phone and listen to them several times throughout your day)*

I am... _____

_____
_____
_____
_____
_____
_____

My two massive goals to focus on today:

1. _____
2. _____

Take three deep "oxytocin breaths" by placing your hand on your heart and exhaling the sound "haaaaa".

My Mind Candy Minute Journal

Date _____/_____/_____

"Nature gave men two ends... one to sit on and one to think with. Ever since then man's success or failure has been dependent on the one he used most." - George R. Kilpatrick

I am grateful for...

1. _____
2. _____
3. _____

Daily affirmations. Mind Candy Voice Note *(Record your affirmations on your smart phone and listen to them several times throughout your day)*

I am... _____

_____
_____
_____
_____
_____
_____

My two massive goals to focus on today:

1. _____
2. _____

Take three deep "oxytocin breaths" by placing your hand on your heart and exhaling the sound "haaaaa".

My Mind Candy Minute Journal

Date ____/____/_____

*"The will to do springs from the knowledge
that we can do." - James Allen*

I am grateful for...

1. _____
2. _____
3. _____

Daily affirmations. Mind Candy Voice Note *(Record your affirmations on your smart phone and listen to them several times throughout your day)*

I am... _____

_____

_____

_____

_____

_____

_____

My two massive goals to focus on today:

1. _____
2. _____

Take three deep "oxytocin breaths" by placing your hand
on your heart and exhaling the sound "haaaaa".

My Mind Candy Minute Journal

Date ____/____/_____

"It is observed that successful people get ahead in the time that other people waste." - Henry Ford

I am grateful for...

1. _____
2. _____
3. _____

Daily affirmations. Mind Candy Voice Note *(Record your affirmations on your smart phone and listen to them several times throughout your day)*

I am... _____

_____
_____
_____
_____
_____
_____

My two massive goals to focus on today:

1. _____
2. _____

Take three deep "oxytocin breaths" by placing your hand on your heart and exhaling the sound "haaaaa".

My Mind Candy Minute Journal

Date ____/____/_____

"You see things and say, 'Why?' But I dream of things that never were and say 'Why not?'" - George Bernard Shaw

I am grateful for...

1. _____
2. _____
3. _____

Daily affirmations. Mind Candy Voice Note *(Record your affirmations on your smart phone and listen to them several times throughout your day)*

I am... _____

_____
_____
_____
_____
_____
_____

My two massive goals to focus on today:

1. _____
2. _____

Take three deep "oxytocin breaths" by placing your hand on your heart and exhaling the sound "haaaaa".

My Mind Candy Minute Journal

Date ____/____/_____

"Many of life's failures are people who did not realize how close they were to success when they gave up." - Thomas Edison

I am grateful for...

1. _____
2. _____
3. _____

Daily affirmations. Mind Candy Voice Note *(Record your affirmations on your smart phone and listen to them several times throughout your day)*

I am... _____

_____
_____
_____
_____
_____
_____

My two massive goals to focus on today:

1. _____
2. _____

Take three deep "oxytocin breaths" by placing your hand on your heart and exhaling the sound "haaaaa".

My Mind Candy Minute Journal

Date ____/____/_____

"You must have long range goals to keep from being frustrated by short-term failures." - Bob Bales

I am grateful for...

1. _____
2. _____
3. _____

Daily affirmations. Mind Candy Voice Note *(Record your affirmations on your smart phone and listen to them several times throughout your day)*

I am... _____

_____
_____
_____
_____
_____
_____

My two massive goals to focus on today:

1. _____
2. _____

Take three deep "oxytocin breaths" by placing your hand on your heart and exhaling the sound "haaaaa".

My Mind Candy Minute Journal

Date ____/____/_____

"I would rather attempt something great and fail than attempt to do nothing and succeed." - Robert Schuller

I am grateful for...

1. _____
2. _____
3. _____

Daily affirmations. Mind Candy Voice Note *(Record your affirmations on your smart phone and listen to them several times throughout your day)*

I am... _____

_____
_____
_____
_____
_____
_____

My two massive goals to focus on today:

1. _____
2. _____

Take three deep "oxytocin breaths" by placing your hand on your heart and exhaling the sound "haaaaa".

My Mind Candy Minute Journal

Date ____/____/_____

"What you can do, or dream you can, begin it. Boldness has genius, power, and magic in it." - Goethe

I am grateful for...

1. _____
2. _____
3. _____

Daily affirmations. Mind Candy Voice Note *(Record your affirmations on your smart phone and listen to them several times throughout your day)*

I am... _____

_____
_____
_____
_____
_____
_____

My two massive goals to focus on today:

1. _____
2. _____

Take three deep "oxytocin breaths" by placing your hand on your heart and exhaling the sound "haaaaa".

My Mind Candy Minute Journal

Date ____/____/_____

"Our lives improve only when we take chances, and the first and most difficult risk we can take is to be honest with ourselves." - Walter Anderson

I am grateful for...

1. _____
2. _____
3. _____

Daily affirmations. Mind Candy Voice Note *(Record your affirmations on your smart phone and listen to them several times throughout your day)*

I am... _____

_____
_____
_____
_____
_____
_____
_____

My two massive goals to focus on today:

1. _____
2. _____

Take three deep "oxytocin breaths" by placing your hand on your heart and exhaling the sound "haaaaa".

My Mind Candy Minute Journal

Date ____/____/_____

"Either do not attempt at all, or go through with it." - Ovid

I am grateful for...

1. _____
2. _____
3. _____

Daily affirmations. Mind Candy Voice Note *(Record your affirmations on your smart phone and listen to them several times throughout your day)*

I am... _____
_____
_____
_____
_____
_____
_____

My two massive goals to focus on today:

1. _____
2. _____

Take three deep "oxytocin breaths" by placing your hand on your heart and exhaling the sound "haaaaa".

My Mind Candy Minute Journal

Date ____/____/_____

"I don't dream at night, I dream all day. I dream for a living." - Steven Spielberg

I am grateful for...

1. _____
2. _____
3. _____

Daily affirmations. Mind Candy Voice Note *(Record your affirmations on your smart phone and listen to them several times throughout your day)*

I am... _____

_____
_____
_____
_____
_____

My two massive goals to focus on today:

1. _____
2. _____

Take three deep "oxytocin breaths" by placing your hand on your heart and exhaling the sound "haaaaa".

My Mind Candy Minute Journal

Date ____/____/_____

"Hope is the companion of power and the mother of success. For those of us who hope strongest have within us the gift of miracles." - Sydney Bremer

I am grateful for...

1. _____
2. _____
3. _____

Daily affirmations. Mind Candy Voice Note *(Record your affirmations on your smart phone and listen to them several times throughout your day)*

I am... _____

_____
_____
_____
_____
_____
_____

My two massive goals to focus on today:

1. _____
2. _____

Take three deep "oxytocin breaths" by placing your hand on your heart and exhaling the sound "haaaaa".

My Mind Candy Minute Journal

Date ____/____/_____

"The gem cannot be polished without friction, nor man perfected without trials." - Confucius

I am grateful for...

1. _____
2. _____
3. _____

Daily affirmations. Mind Candy Voice Note *(Record your affirmations on your smart phone and listen to them several times throughout your day)*

I am... _____

_____
_____
_____
_____
_____
_____

My two massive goals to focus on today:

1. _____
2. _____

Take three deep "oxytocin breaths" by placing your hand on your heart and exhaling the sound "haaaaa".

My Mind Candy Minute Journal

Date ____/____/_____

"If you don't know where you are going, every road will get you nowhere." - Henry Kissinger

I am grateful for...

1. _____
2. _____
3. _____

Daily affirmations. Mind Candy Voice Note *(Record your affirmations on your smart phone and listen to them several times throughout your day)*

I am... _____

_____
_____
_____
_____
_____
_____

My two massive goals to focus on today:

1. _____
2. _____

Take three deep "oxytocin breaths" by placing your hand on your heart and exhaling the sound "haaaaa".

My Mind Candy Minute Journal

Date ____/____/_____

"Man is what he believes." - Anton Chekhov

I am grateful for...

1. _____
2. _____
3. _____

Daily affirmations. Mind Candy Voice Note *(Record your affirmations on your smart phone and listen to them several times throughout your day)*

I am... _____

_____
_____
_____
_____
_____
_____

My two massive goals to focus on today:

1. _____
2. _____

Take three deep "oxytocin breaths" by placing your hand on your heart and exhaling the sound "haaaaa".

My Mind Candy Minute Journal

Date ____/____/_____

"Goals are dreams we convert to plans and take action to fulfill." - Zig Ziglar

I am grateful for...

1. _____
2. _____
3. _____

Daily affirmations. Mind Candy Voice Note *(Record your affirmations on your smart phone and listen to them several times throughout your day)*

I am... _____

_____
_____
_____
_____
_____
_____

My two massive goals to focus on today:

1. _____
2. _____

Take three deep "oxytocin breaths" by placing your hand on your heart and exhaling the sound "haaaaa".

My Mind Candy Minute Journal

Date ____/____/_____

"Four steps to achievement: plan purposefully, prepare prayerfully, proceed positively, pursue persistently." - William A. Ward

I am grateful for...

1. _____
2. _____
3. _____

Daily affirmations. Mind Candy Voice Note *(Record your affirmations on your smart phone and listen to them several times throughout your day)*

I am... _____

_____
_____
_____
_____
_____
_____

My two massive goals to focus on today:

1. _____
2. _____

Take three deep "oxytocin breaths" by placing your hand on your heart and exhaling the sound "haaaaa".

My Mind Candy Minute Journal

Date ____/____/_____

"I never waste time looking back." - Eleanor Roosevelt

I am grateful for...

1. _____
2. _____
3. _____

Daily affirmations. Mind Candy Voice Note *(Record your affirmations on your smart phone and listen to them several times throughout your day)*

I am... _____

_____

_____

_____

_____

_____

My two massive goals to focus on today:

1. _____
2. _____

Take three deep "oxytocin breaths" by placing your hand on your heart and exhaling the sound "haaaaa".

My Mind Candy Minute Journal

Date ____/____/_____

"Who told you it couldn't be done? And what great achievement has he to his credit that entitles him to use the word 'impossible' so freely?" - Napoleon Hill

I am grateful for...

1. _____
2. _____
3. _____

Daily affirmations. Mind Candy Voice Note *(Record your affirmations on your smart phone and listen to them several times throughout your day)*

I am... _____

_____
_____
_____
_____
_____
_____

My two massive goals to focus on today:

1. _____
2. _____

Take three deep "oxytocin breaths" by placing your hand on your heart and exhaling the sound "haaaaa".

My Mind Candy Minute Journal

Date ____/____/_____

"Dream no small dreams for they have no power to move the hearts of men." - Goethe

I am grateful for...

1. _____
2. _____
3. _____

Daily affirmations. Mind Candy Voice Note *(Record your affirmations on your smart phone and listen to them several times throughout your day)*

I am... _____

_____
_____
_____
_____
_____
_____

My two massive goals to focus on today:

1. _____
2. _____

Take three deep "oxytocin breaths" by placing your hand on your heart and exhaling the sound "haaaaa".

My Mind Candy Minute Journal

Date ____/____/_____

"I am a slow walker ... but I never walk backwards." - Abraham Lincoln

I am grateful for...

1. _____
2. _____
3. _____

Daily affirmations. Mind Candy Voice Note *(Record your affirmations on your smart phone and listen to them several times throughout your day)*

I am... _____

_____
_____
_____
_____
_____
_____

My two massive goals to focus on today:

1. _____
2. _____

Take three deep "oxytocin breaths" by placing your hand on your heart and exhaling the sound "haaaaa".

My Mind Candy Minute Journal

Date ____/____/_____

"An aim in life is the only fortune worth finding, and it is not to be found in foreign lands, but in the heart itself." - Robert Louis Stevenson

I am grateful for...

1. _____
2. _____
3. _____

Daily affirmations. Mind Candy Voice Note *(Record your affirmations on your smart phone and listen to them several times throughout your day)*

I am... _____
_____
_____
_____
_____
_____
_____

My two massive goals to focus on today:

1. _____
2. _____

Take three deep "oxytocin breaths" by placing your hand on your heart and exhaling the sound "haaaaa".

My Mind Candy Minute Journal

Date _____/_____/_____

"Wherever you see a successful business, someone once made a courageous decision." - Peter F. Drucker

I am grateful for...

1. _____
2. _____
3. _____

Daily affirmations. Mind Candy Voice Note *(Record your affirmations on your smart phone and listen to them several times throughout your day)*

I am... _____

_____
_____
_____
_____
_____
_____

My two massive goals to focus on today:

1. _____
2. _____

Take three deep "oxytocin breaths" by placing your hand on your heart and exhaling the sound "haaaaa".

My Mind Candy Minute Journal

Date ____/____/_____

"The road to success runs uphill." - Willie Davis

I am grateful for...

1. _____
2. _____
3. _____

Daily affirmations. Mind Candy Voice Note *(Record your affirmations on your smart phone and listen to them several times throughout your day)*

I am... _____

_____

_____

_____

_____

_____

My two massive goals to focus on today:

1. _____
2. _____

Take three deep "oxytocin breaths" by placing your hand on your heart and exhaling the sound "haaaaa".

My Mind Candy Minute Journal

Date ____/____/_____

"Success requires first expending ten units of effort to produce one unit of results. Your momentum will then produce ten units of results with each unit of effort." - Charles Givens

I am grateful for...

1. _____
2. _____
3. _____

Daily affirmations. Mind Candy Voice Note *(Record your affirmations on your smart phone and listen to them several times throughout your day)*

I am... _____
_____
_____
_____
_____
_____
_____

My two massive goals to focus on today:

1. _____
2. _____

Take three deep "oxytocin breaths" by placing your hand on your heart and exhaling the sound "haaaaa".

My Mind Candy Minute Journal

Date ____/____/_____

"The only honest measure of your success is what you are doing compared to your true potential." - Paul J. Meyer

I am grateful for...

1. _____
2. _____
3. _____

Daily affirmations. Mind Candy Voice Note *(Record your affirmations on your smart phone and listen to them several times throughout your day)*

I am... _____
_____
_____
_____
_____
_____
_____

My two massive goals to focus on today:

1. _____
2. _____

Take three deep "oxytocin breaths" by placing your hand on your heart and exhaling the sound "haaaaa".

My Mind Candy Minute Journal

Date ____/____/_____

"Any fact facing us is not as important as our attitude toward it, for that determines our success or failure." - Norman Vincent Peale

I am grateful for...

1. _____
2. _____
3. _____

Daily affirmations. Mind Candy Voice Note *(Record your affirmations on your smart phone and listen to them several times throughout your day)*

I am... _____

_____
_____
_____
_____
_____
_____
_____

My two massive goals to focus on today:

1. _____
2. _____

Take three deep "oxytocin breaths" by placing your hand on your heart and exhaling the sound "haaaaa".

My Mind Candy Minute Journal

Date ____/____/_____

FGHIJKLMNOPQRSTUVWXYZ~!@#$%^&*()_+|1234567890-=\
[];',./{}:"<>?

I am grateful for...

1. _____
2. _____
3. _____

Daily affirmations. Mind Candy Voice Note *(Record your affirmations on your smart phone and listen to them several times throughout your day)*

I am... _____

_____
_____
_____
_____
_____
_____

My two massive goals to focus on today:

1. _____
2. _____

Take three deep "oxytocin breaths" by placing your hand on your heart and exhaling the sound "haaaaa".

My Mind Candy Minute Journal

Date ____/____/_____

"It is easy to sit up and take notice. What is difficult is getting up and taking action." - Al Batt

I am grateful for...

1. _____
2. _____
3. _____

Daily affirmations. Mind Candy Voice Note *(Record your affirmations on your smart phone and listen to them several times throughout your day)*

I am... _____

_____
_____
_____
_____
_____
_____

My two massive goals to focus on today:

1. _____
2. _____

Take three deep "oxytocin breaths" by placing your hand on your heart and exhaling the sound "haaaaa".

My Mind Candy Minute Journal

Date ____/____/_____

"Success is getting what you want. Happiness is wanting what you get." - Dale Carnegie

I am grateful for...

1. _____
2. _____
3. _____

Daily affirmations. Mind Candy Voice Note *(Record your affirmations on your smart phone and listen to them several times throughout your day)*

I am... _____
_____
_____
_____
_____
_____
_____

My two massive goals to focus on today:

1. _____
2. _____

Take three deep "oxytocin breaths" by placing your hand on your heart and exhaling the sound "haaaaa".

My Mind Candy Minute Journal

Date ____/____/_____

"Never, never, never, never give up." - Winston Churchill

I am grateful for...

1. _____
2. _____
3. _____

Daily affirmations. Mind Candy Voice Note *(Record your affirmations on your smart phone and listen to them several times throughout your day)*

I am... _____

_____
_____
_____
_____
_____
_____

My two massive goals to focus on today:

1. _____
2. _____

Take three deep "oxytocin breaths" by placing your hand on your heart and exhaling the sound "haaaaa".

My Mind Candy Minute Journal

Date ____/____/_____

"Ones best success comes after their greatest disappointments." - Henry Ward Beecher

I am grateful for...

1. _____
2. _____
3. _____

Daily affirmations. Mind Candy Voice Note *(Record your affirmations on your smart phone and listen to them several times throughout your day)*

I am... _____

_____

_____

_____

_____

_____

_____

My two massive goals to focus on today:

1. _____
2. _____

Take three deep "oxytocin breaths" by placing your hand on your heart and exhaling the sound "haaaaa".

My Mind Candy Minute Journal

Date ____/____/_____

"Nothing in the world can take the place of persistence. Talent will not; nothing is more common than unsuccessful men with talent. Genius will not; the world is full of educated derelicts. Persistence and determination alone are omnipotent. The phrase 'press on' has solved and always will solve the problems of the human race." - Calvin Coolidge

I am grateful for...

1. _____
2. _____
3. _____

Daily affirmations. Mind Candy Voice Note *(Record your affirmations on your smart phone and listen to them several times throughout your day)*

I am... _____

_____
_____
_____
_____
_____
_____

My two massive goals to focus on today:

1. _____
2. _____

Take three deep "oxytocin breaths" by placing your hand on your heart and exhaling the sound "haaaaa".

RECOMMENDED RESOURCES

GET PUBLISHED!

The Ultimate Publishing House's Production System is so precise, we can have your book released in 6 months:

All of our book publishing programs include:

- mastermind session
- personal project manager
- professional ghostwriter
- five phases of editing
- branded book website
- worldwide distribution
- marketing
- publicity
- media coaching
- book cover design
- image consulting

And much more!
UPH is here to make your book publishing dreams come true!

CALL TODAY TO START YOUR BOOK, IT IS THE BEST MARKETING INVESTMENT YOU WILL EVER MAKE!

647 883 1758 OR Email: author@ultimatepublishinghouse.com

The publishing world has changed dramatically. In the new economy with global opportunities, you are either distinct or extinct, the choice is yours.

A BOOK IS THE ULTIMATE BRANDING TOOL THAT OFFERS:

- Credibility
- Visibility
- Distinction
- Positions you as the expert in your field
- Media exposure
- Attract more clients or patients
- Opportunities for product endorsements
- It's time you publish your own book with the Ultimate Publishing House!

www.ultimatepublishinghouse.com

ilovemyhormones.tv

GET LISTED!

ilovemyhormones.tv is the PERFECT marketing tool to advertise yourself and your practice. We invite you to utilize our website as a platform and catalyst to increase your visibility, credibility, and distinction which ultimately enables your practice to attract more patients.

The opportunities are endless. The KEY to SUCCESSFUL marketing is knowing your target market and being able to pinpoint it. This is exactly what **ilovemyhormones.tv** does for you.

For only $2,000.00 pet annum, your ROI is guaranteed with as little as one new patient.

Enhanced Listing Delivers:

- 3 times more leads than the basic listing.
- 2 free editorials per year to spotlight you and your practice.
- 500 word biography to best describe your products and services to our readers.
- Premium listing position within the directory for your state/province.
- Your own personal page, direct hyperlink from our directory.
- A variety of options within the page: company overview, photo gallery, practice specialties, editorial, ability to promote your services and products.
- Qualified patients/leads with a single click, direct access to your office via e-mail hyperlink.
- Featured on homepage in "Today's Feature" next to Dr. Oz & Oprah.
- Qualified leads with a single click, readers can request information directly from you.

Contact us today to get started at
advertise@ilovemyhormones.tv or call **647.883.1758**

The Ultimate Program for Youth & Teens
to Say YES to Their Dreams!

Youth Entrepreneurship School

THE ULTIMATE SCHOOL THAT TEACHES OUR YOUTH HOW TO LIVE FROM THEIR HEARTS.

Y.E.S. PROVIDES STUDENTS WTIH THE SKILLS & MINDSET REQUIRED TO RUN ANY BUSINESS & ACHIEVE FULFILLMENT!

Founder: Felicia Pizzonia, Publisher & Best Selling Author
direct email: info@ultimatepublishinghouse.com

PERSONAL COACHING

WITH FELICIA PIZZONIA

We will visit on the phone, FaceTime, Skype or in person for a half hour. During our visit we will determine if you are "coachable." I can't know for sure if we will be a good match but even if we're not, I guarantee one thing. After we're through visiting, your entire way of looking at life and how you live from your heart and ultimately the way you earn money will change FOREVER!

Following is a snapshot of the things you'll learn during our coaching sessions:

1. What is it that you truly desire to achieve in your life?
2. What are your three highest values in life and how to live the life you desire. Your life is a reflection of your three highest values. I will help you determine them and live from your heart.
3. Are you willing to take massive, calculated action to rewire your brain for success?
4. How to use the science of closing sales in order to double or triple your annual sales revenue by using my proven methods. (scienceofclosingsales.com)

...and PLENTY MORE!

Contact: Felicia Pizzonia
FeliciaPizzonia.com
Coaching@MindCandy.com
Phone: 647 883 1758

HEARTCORE HUSTLE

2019 BOOK RELEASE

Pre-oder your copy at www.FeliciaPizzonia.com
How to live from your heart to achieve massive success.

ONLY $29.97

www.ingramcontent.com/pod-product-compliance
Lightning Source LLC
Chambersburg PA
CBHW072001150426
43194CB00008B/960